In Morocco

In Morocco
by Edith Wharton

©2015 SMK Books

Wilder Publications, LLC.
PO Box 3005
Radford VA 24143-3005

ISBN 13: 978-1-5154-0138-4

Table of Contents:

PREFACE

I

Having begun my book with the statement that Morocco still lacks aguide-book, I should have wished to take a first step toward remedyingthat deficiency.

But the conditions in which I travelled, though full of unexpected andpicturesque opportunities, were not suited to leisurely study of theplaces visited. The time was limited by the approach of the rainyseason, which puts an end to motoring over the treacherous trails of theSpanish zone. In 1918, owing to the watchfulness of German submarines inthe Straits and along the northwest coast of Africa, the trip by seafrom Marseilles to Casablanca, ordinarily so easy, was not to be madewithout much discomfort and loss of time. Once on board the steamer,passengers were often kept in port (without leave to land) for six oreight days; therefore for any one bound by a time-limit, as mostwar-workers were, it was necessary to travel across country, and to beback at Tangier before the November rains.

This left me only one month in which to visit Morocco from theMediterranean to the High Atlas, and from the Atlantic to Fez, and evenhad there been a Djinn's carpet to carry me, the multiplicity ofimpressions received would have made precise observation difficult.

The next best thing to a Djinn's carpet, a military motor, was at mydisposal every morning; but war conditions imposed restrictions, and thewish to use the minimum of petrol often stood in the way of the secondvisit which alone makes it possible to carry away a definite anddetailed impression.

These drawbacks were more than offset by the advantage of making myquick trip at a moment unique in the history of the country; the briefmoment of transition between its virtually complete subjection toEuropean authority, and the fast approaching hour when it is thrown opento all the banalities and promiscuities of modern travel.

Morocco is too curious, too beautiful, too rich in landscape andarchitecture, and above all too much of a novelty, not to attract one ofthe main streams of spring travel as soon as Mediterranean passengertraffic is resumed. Now that the war is over, only a few months' work onroads and railways divide it from the great torrent of "tourism"; andonce that deluge is let loose, no eye will ever again see Moulay Idrissand Fez and Marrakech as I saw them.

In spite of the incessant efforts of the present French administrationto preserve the old monuments of Morocco from injury, and her nativearts and industries from the corruption of European bad taste, theimpression of mystery and remoteness which the country now produces mustinevitably vanish with the approach of the "Circular Ticket." Within afew years far more will be known of the past of Morocco, but that pastwill be far less visible to the traveller than it is to-day. Excavationswill reveal fresh traces of Roman and Phenician occupation; the remoteaffinities between Copts and Berbers, between Bagdad and Fez, betweenByzantine art and the architecture of the Souss, will be explored andelucidated; but, while these successive discoveries are being made, thestrange survival of mediæval life, of a life contemporary with thecrusaders, with Saladin, even with the great days of the Caliphate ofBagdad, which now greets the astonished traveller, will graduallydisappear, till at last even the mysterious autocthones of the Atlaswill have folded their tents and silently stolen away.

II

Authoritative utterances on Morocco are not wanting for those who canread them in French; but they are to be found mainly in large and ofteninaccessible books, like M. Doutté's "En Tribu," the Marquis deSegonzac's remarkable explorations in the Atlas, or Foucauld's classic(but unobtainable) "Reconnaissance au Maroc"; and few, if any, have beentranslated into English.

M. Louis Châtelain has dealt with the Roman ruins of Volubilis and M.Tranchant de Lunel, M. Raymond Koechlin, M. Gaillard, M. Ricard, andmany other French scholars, have written of Moslem architecture and artin articles published either in "France-Maroc," as introductions tocatalogues of exhibitions, or in the reviews and daily papers. PierreLoti and M. André Chevrillon have reflected, with the intensest visualsensibility, the romantic and ruinous Morocco of yesterday; and in thevolumes of the "Conférences Marocaines," published by the Frenchgovernment, the experts gathered about the Resident-General haveexamined the industrial and agricultural Morocco of to-morrow. Lastly,one striking book sums up, with the clearness and consecutiveness ofwhich French scholarship alone possesses the art, the chief things to besaid on all these subjects, save that of art and archæology. This is M.Augustin Bernard's volume, "Le Maroc," the one portable and compact yetfull and informing book since Leo Africanus described the bazaars ofFez. But M. Augustin Bernard deals only with the ethnology, the social,religious and political history, and the physical properties, of thecountry; and this, though "a large order," leaves out the visual andpicturesque side, except in so far as the book touches on the alwayspicturesque life of the people.

For the use, therefore, of the happy wanderers who may be planning aMoroccan journey, I have added to the record of my personal impressionsa slight sketch of the history and art of the country. In extenuation ofthe attempt I must add that the chief merit of this sketch will be itsabsence of originality. Its facts will be chiefly drawn from the pagesof M. Augustin Bernard, M. H. Saladin, and M. Gaston Migeon, and therich sources of the "Conférences Marocaines" and the articles of"France-Maroc." It will also be deeply indebted to information given onthe spot by the brilliant specialists of the French administration, tothe Marquis de Segonzac, with whom I had the good luck to travel fromRabat to Marrakech and back; to M. Alfred de Tarde, editor of"France-Maroc"; to M. Tranchant de Lunel, director of the French Schoolof Fine Arts in Morocco; to M. Goulven, the historian of PortugueseMazagan; to M. Louis Châtelain, and to the many other cultivated andcordial French officials, military and civilian, who, at each stage ofmy journey, did their amiable best to answer my questions and open myeyes.

I
RABAT AND SALÉ

I

LEAVING TANGIER

To step on board a steamer in a Spanish port, and three hours later toland in *a country without a guide-book*, is a sensation to rouse thehunger of the repletest sight-seer.

The sensation is attainable by any one who will take the trouble to rowout into the harbour of Algeciras and scramble onto a little black boatheaded across the straits. Hardly has the rock of Gibraltar turned tocloud when one's foot is on the soil of an almost unknown Africa.Tangier, indeed, is in the guide-books; but, cuckoo-like, it has had tolays its egg in strange nests, and the traveller who wants to find outabout it must acquire a work dealing with some other country—Spain orPortugal or Algeria. There is no guide-book to Morocco, and no way ofknowing, once one has left Tangier behind, where the long trail over theRif is going to land one, in the sense understood by any one accustomedto European certainties. The air of the unforeseen blows on one from theroadless passes of the Atlas.

This feeling of adventure is heightened by the contrast betweenTangier—cosmopolitan, frowsy, familiar Tangier, that every tourist hasvisited for the last forty years—and the vast unknown just beyond. Onehas met, of course, travellers who have been to Fez; but they have gonethere on special missions, under escort, mysteriously, perhapsperilously; the expedition has seemed, till lately, a considerableaffair. And when one opens the records of Moroccan travellers writtenwithin the last twenty years, how many, even of the most adventurous,are found to have gone beyond Fez? And what, to this day, do the namesof Meknez and Marrakech, of Mogador, Saffi or Rabat, signify to any buta few students of political history, a few explorers and naturalists?Not till within the last year has Morocco been open to travel fromTangier to the Great Atlas, and from Moulay Idriss to the Atlantic.Three years ago Christians were being massacred in the streets of Salé,the pirate town across the river from Rabat, and two years ago noEuropean had been allowed to enter the Sacred City of Moulay Idriss, theburial-place of the lawful descendant of Ali, founder of the Idrissitedynasty. Now, thanks to the energy and the imagination of one of thegreatest of colonial administrators, the country, at least in the Frenchzone, is as safe and open as the opposite shore of Spain. All thatremains is to tell the traveller how to find his way about it.

Ten years ago there was not a wheeled vehicle in Morocco; now itsthousands of miles of trail, and its hundreds of miles of firm Frenchroads, are travelled by countless carts, omnibuses and motor-vehicles.There are light railways from Rabat to Fez in the west, and to a pointabout eighty-five kilometres from Marrakech in the south; and it ispossible to say that within a year a regular railway system will connecteastern Morocco with western Algeria, and the ports of Tangier andCasablanca with the principal points of the interior.

What, then, prevents the tourist from instantly taking ship at Bordeauxor Algeciras and letting loose his motor on this new world? Only thetemporary obstacles which the war has everywhere put in the way oftravel. Till these are lifted it will hardly be possible to travel inMorocco except by favour of the Resident-General; but, normal conditionsonce restored, the country will be as accessible, from the straits ofGibraltar to the Great Atlas, as Algeria or Tunisia.

To see Morocco during the war was therefore to see it in the last phaseof its curiously abrupt transition from remoteness and danger tosecurity and accessibility; at a moment when its aspect and its customswere still almost unaffected by European influences, and when the"Christian" might taste the transient joy of wandering unmolested incities of ancient mystery and hostility, whose inhabitants seemed hardlyaware of his intrusion.

II

THE TRAIL TO EL-KSAR

With such opportunities ahead it was impossible, that brilliant morningof September, 1917, not to be off quickly from Tangier, impossible to dojustice to the pale-blue town piled up within brown walls against thethickly-foliaged gardens of "the Mountain," to the animation ofitsmarket-place and the secret beauties of its steep Arab streets. ForTangier swarms with people in European clothes, there are English,French and Spanish signs above its shops, and cab-stands in its squares;it belongs, as much as Algiers, to the familiar dog-eared world oftravel—and there, beyond the last dip of "the Mountain," lies the worldof mystery, with the rosy dawn just breaking over it. The motor is atthe door and we are off.

The so-called Spanish zone, which encloses internationalized Tangier ina wide circuit of territory, extends southward for a distance of about ahundred and fifteen kilometres. Consequently, when good roads traverseit, French Morocco will be reached in less than two hours bymotor-travellers bound for the south. But for the present Spanishenterprise dies out after a few miles of macadam (as it does evenbetween Madrid and Toledo), and the tourist is committed to the *piste*.These *pistes*—the old caravan-trails from the south—are moreavailable to motors in Morocco than in southern Algeria and Tunisia,since they run mostly over soil which, though sandy in part, is boundtogether by a tough dwarf vegetation, and not over pure desert sand.This, however, is the utmost that can be said of the Spanish *pistes*.In the French protectorate constant efforts are made to keep the trailsfit for wheeled traffic, but Spain shows no sense of a correspondingobligation.

After leaving the macadamized road which runs south from Tangier oneseems to have embarked on a petrified ocean in a boat hardly equal tothe adventure. Then, as one leaps and plunges over humps and ruts, downsheer banks into rivers, and up precipices into sand-pits, one graduallygains faith in one's conveyance and in one's spinal column; but bothmust be sound in every joint to resist the strain of the long miles toArbaoua, the frontier post of the French protectorate.

Luckily there are other things to think about. At the first turn out ofTangier, Europe and the European disappear, and as soon as the motorbegins to dip and rise over the arid little hills beyond to the lastgardens one is sure that every figure on the road will be picturesqueinstead of prosaic, every garment graceful instead of grotesque. Oneknows, too, that there will be no more omnibuses or trams ormotorcyclists, but only long lines of camels rising up in brown friezesagainst the sky, little black donkeys trotting across the scrub underbulging pack-saddles, and noble draped figures walking beside them ormajestically perching on their rumps. And for miles and miles there willbe no more towns—only, at intervals on the naked slopes, circles ofrush-roofed huts in a blue stockade of cactus, or a hundred or two nomadtents of black camel's hair resting on walls of wattled thorn andgrouped about a terebinth-tree and a well.

Between these nomad colonies lies the *bled*, the immense waste offallow land and palmetto desert: an earth as void of life as the skyabove it of clouds. The scenery is always the same; but if one has thelove of great emptinesses, and of the play of light on long stretches ofparched earth and rock, the sameness is part of the enchantment. In sucha scene every landmark takes on an extreme value. For miles one watchesthe little white dome of a saint's grave rising and disappearing withthe undulations of the trail; at last one is abreast of it, and thesolitary tomb, alone with its fig-tree and its broken well-curb, puts ameaning into the waste. The same importance, but intensified, marks theappearance of every human figure. The two white-draped riders passingsingle file up the red slope to that ring of tents on the ridge have amysterious and inexplicable importance: one follows their progress witheyes that ache with conjecture. More exciting still is the encounter ofthe first veiled woman heading a little cavalcade from the south. Allthe mystery that awaits us looks out through the eye-slits in thegrave-clothes muffling her. Where have they come from, where are theygoing, all these slow wayfarers out of the unknown? Probably only fromone thatched *douar* to another; but interminable distances unrollbehind them, they breathe of Timbuctoo and the farthest desert. Justsuch figures must swarm in the Saharan cities, in the Soudan andSenegal. There is no break in the links: these wanderers have looked onat the building of cities that were dust when the Romans pushed theiroutposts across the Atlas.

III

EL-KSAR TO RABAT

A town at last—its nearness announced by the multiplied ruts of thetrail, the cactus hedges, the fig-trees weighed down by dust leaningover ruinous earthern walls. And here are the first houses of theEuropean El-Ksar—neat white Spanish houses on the slope outside the oldArab settlement. Of the Arab town itself, above reed stockades and brownwalls, only a minaret and a few flat roofs are visible. Under the wallsdrowse the usual gregarious

Lazaruses; others, temporarily resuscitated, trail their grave-clothes after a line of camels and donkeys toward the olive-gardens outside the town.

The way to Rabat is long and difficult, and there is no time to visit El-Ksar, though its minaret beckons so alluringly above the fruit-orchards; so we stop for luncheon outside the walls, at a canteen with a corrugated iron roof where skinny Spaniards are serving thick purple wine and eggs fried in oil to a party of French soldiers. The heat has suddenly become intolerable, and a flaming wind straight from the south brings in at the door, with a cloud of blue flies, the smell of camels and trampled herbs and the strong spices of the bazaars.

Luncheon over, we hurry on between the cactus hedges, and then plunge back into the waste. Beyond El-Ksar the last hills of the Rif die away, and there is a stretch of wilderness without an outline till the Lesser Atlas begins to rise in the east. Once in the French protectorate the trail improves, but there are still difficult bits; and finally, on a high plateau, the chauffeur stops in a web of crisscross trails, throws up his hands, and confesses that he has lost his way. The heat is mortal at the moment. For the last hour the red breath of the sirocco has risen from every hollow into which we dipped; now it hangs about us in the open, as if we had caught it in our wheels and it had to pause above us when we paused.

All around is the featureless wild land, palmetto scrub stretching away into eternity. A few yards off rises the inevitable ruined *koubba* with its fig-tree: in the shade under its crumbling wall the buzz of the flies is like the sound of frying. Farther off, we discern a cluster of huts, and presently some Arab boys and a tall pensive shepherd come hurrying across the scrub. They are full of good-will, and no doubt of information; but our chauffeur speaks no Arabic and the talk dies down into shrugs and head-shakings. The Arabs retire to the shade of the wall, and we decide to start—for anywhere....

The chauffeur turns the crank, but there is no responding quiver. Something has gone wrong; we can't move, and it is not much comfort to remember that, if we could, we should not know where to go. At least we should be cooler in motion than sitting still under the blinding sky.

Such an adventure initiates one at the outset into the stern facts of desert motoring. Every detail of our trip from Tangier to Rabat had been carefully planned to keep us in unbroken contact with civilization. We were to "tub" in one European hotel, and to dine in another, with just enough picnicking between to give a touch of local colour. But let onelittle cog slip and the whole plan falls to bits, and we are alone inthe old untamed Moghreb, as remote from Europe as any mediævaladventurer. If one lose one's way in Morocco, civilization vanishes asthough it were a magic carpet rolled up by a Djinn.

It is a good thing to begin with such a mishap, not only because itdevelops the fatalism necessary to the enjoyment of Africa, but becauseit lets one at once into the mysterious heart of the country: a countryso deeply conditioned by its miles and miles of uncitied wilderness thatuntil one has known the wilderness one cannot begin to understand thecities.

We came to one at length, after sunset on that first endless day. Themotor, cleverly patched up, had found its way to a real road, andspeeding along between the stunted cork-trees of the forest of Mamorabrought us to a last rise from which we beheld in the dusk a line ofyellow walls backed by the misty blue of the Atlantic. Salé, the fierceold pirate town, where Robinson Crusoe was so long a slave, lay beforeus, snow-white in its cheese-coloured ramparts skirted by fig and olivegardens. Below its gates a stretch of waste land, endlessly trailed overby mules and camels, sloped down to the mouth of the Bou-Regreg, theblue-brown river dividing it from Rabat. The motor stopped at thelanding-stage of the steam-ferry; crowding about it were droves ofdonkeys, knots of camels, plump-faced merchants on crimson-saddledmules, with negro servants at their bridles, bare-legged water-carrierswith hairy goat-skins slung over their shoulders, and Arab women in aheap of veils, cloaks, mufflings, all of the same ashy white, thecaftans of clutched children peeping through in patches of old rose andlilac and pale green.

Across the river the native town of Rabat lay piled up on an orange-redcliff beaten by the Atlantic. Its walls, red too, plunged into thedarkening breakers at the mouth of the river; and behind it, stretchingup to the mighty tower of Hassan, and the ruins of the Great Mosque, thescattered houses of the European city showed their many lights acrossthe plain.

IV

THE KASBAH OF THE OUDAYAS

Salé the white and Rabat the red frown at each other over the foamingbar of the Bou-Regreg, each walled, terraced, minareted, and presentinga singularly complete picture of the two types of Moroccan town, thesnowy and the tawny. To the gates of both the Atlantic breakers roll inwith the boom of northern seas, and under a misty northern sky. It isone of the surprises of Morocco to find the familiar African picturesbathed in this unfamiliar haze. Even the fierce midday sun does notwholly dispel it: the air remains thick, opalescent, like water slightlyclouded by milk. One is tempted to say that Morocco is Tunisia seen bymoonlight.

The European town of Rabat, a rapidly developing community, lies almostwholly outside the walls of the old Arab city. The latter, founded inthe twelfth century by the great Almohad conqueror of Spain, Yacoub-el-Mansour, stretches its mighty walls to the river's mouth. Thence they climb the cliff to enclose the Kasbah of the Oudayas, atroublesome tribe whom one of the Almohad Sultans, mistrusting theirgood faith, packed up one day, flocks, tents and camels, and carriedacross the *bled* to stow them into these stout walls under hisimperial eye. Great crenellated ramparts, cyclopean, superb, follow thecurve of the cliff. On the landward side they are interrupted by agate-tower resting on one of the most nobly decorated of the horseshoearches that break the mighty walls of Moroccan cities. Underneath thetower the vaulted entrance turns, Arab fashion, at right angles,profiling its red arch against darkness and mystery. This bending ofpassages, so characteristic a device of the Moroccan builder, is like anarchitectural expression of the tortuous secret soul of the land.

Outside the Kasbah a narrow foot-path is squeezed between the walls andthe edge of the cliff. Toward sunset it looks down on a strange scene.To the south of the citadel the cliff descends to a long dune sloping toa sand-beach; and dune and beach are covered with the slantingheadstones of the immense Arab cemetery of El Alou. Acres and acres ofgraves fall away from the red ramparts to the grey sea; and breakersrolling straight from America send their spray across the lowest stones.

There are always things going on toward evening in an Arab cemetery. Inthis one, travellers from the *bled* are camping in one corner, donkeysgrazing (on heaven knows what), a camel dozing under its pack; inanother, about a new-made grave, there are ritual movements of muffledfigures and wailings of a funeral hymn half drowned by the waves. Nearus, on a fallen headstone, a man with a thoughtful face sits chattingwith two friends and hugging to his breast a tiny boy who looks like agrasshopper in his green caftan; a little way off, a solitaryphilosopher, his eye fixed on the sunset, lies on another grave, smokinghis long pipe of kif.

There is infinite sadness in this scene under the fading sky, beside thecold welter of the Atlantic. One seems to be not in Africa itself, butin the Africa that northern crusaders may have dreamed of in snow-boundcastles by colder shores of the same ocean. This is what Moghreb musthave looked like to the confused imagination of the Middle Ages, toNorman knights burning to ransom the Holy Places, or Hansa merchantsdevising, in steep-roofed towns, of Barbary and the long caravansbringing apes and gold-powder from the south.

*　　*　　*　　*　　*

Inside the gate of the Kasbah one comes on more waste land and on otherwalls—for all Moroccan towns are enclosed in circuit within circuit ofbattlemented masonry. Then, unexpectedly, a gate in one of the innerwalls lets one into a tiled court enclosed in a traceried cloister andoverlooking an orange-grove that rises out of a carpet of roses. Thispeaceful and well-ordered place is the interior of the Medersa (thecollege) of the Oudayas. Morocco is full of these colleges, or ratherlodging-houses of the students frequenting the mosques; for allMahometan education is given in the mosque itself, only the preparatorywork being done in the colleges. The most beautiful of the Medersas datefrom the earlier years of the long Merinid dynasty (1248-1548), theperiod at which Moroccan art, freed from too distinctively Spanish andArab influences, began to develop a delicate grace of its own as farremoved from the extravagance of Spanish ornament as from theinheritance of Roman-Byzantine motives that the first Moslem invasionhad brought with it from Syria and Mesopotamia.

These exquisite collegiate buildings, though still in use whenever theyare near a well-known mosque, have all fallen into a state of sordiddisrepair. The Moroccan Arab, though he continues to build—andfortunately to build in the old tradition, which has never beenlost—has, like all Orientals, an invincible repugnance to repairing andrestoring, and one after another the frail exposed Arab structures, withtheir open courts and badly constructed terrace-roofs, are crumblinginto ruin. Happily the French Government has at last been asked tointervene, and all over Morocco the Medersas are being repaired withskill and discretion. That of the Oudayas is already completelyrestored, and as it had long fallen into disuse it has been transformedby the Ministry of Fine Arts into a museum of Moroccan art.

The plan of the Medersas is always much the same: the eternal plan ofthe Arab house, built about one or more arcaded courts, with long narrowrooms enclosing them on the ground floor, and several stories above,reached by narrow stairs, and often opening on finely carved cedargalleries. The chief difference between the Medersa and the privatehouse, or even the *fondak*, lies in the use to which the rooms areput. In the Medersas, one of the ground-floor apartments is alwaysfitted up as a chapel, and shut off from the court by carved cedar doorsstill often touched with old gilding and vermilion. There are always afew students praying in the chapel, while others sit in the doors of theupper rooms, their books on their knees, or lean over the carvedgalleries chatting with their companions who are washing their feet atthe marble fountain in the court, preparatory to entering the chapel.

In the Medersa of the Oudayas, these native activities have beenreplaced by the lifeless hush of a museum. The rooms are furnished withold rugs, pottery, brasses, the curious embroidered hangings which linethe tents of the chiefs, and other specimens of Arab art. One roomreproduces a barber's shop in the bazaar, its benches covered with finematting, the hanging mirror inlaid with mother-of-pearl, therazor-handles of silver *niello*. The horseshoe arches of the outergallery look out on orange-blossoms, roses and the sea. It is allbeautiful, calm and harmonious; and if one is tempted to mourn theabsence of life and local colour, one has only to visit an abandonedMedersa to see that, but for French intervention, the charmingcolonnades and cedar chambers of the college of the Oudayas would bythis time be a heap of undistinguished rubbish—for plaster and rubbledo not "die in beauty" like the firm stones of Rome.

V

ROBINSON CRUSOE'S "SALLEE"

Before Morocco passed under the rule of the great governor who nowadministers it, the European colonists made short work of the beauty andprivacy of the old Arab towns in which they established themselves.

On the west coast, especially, where the Mediterranean peoples, from thePhenicians to the Portuguese, have had trading-posts for over twothousand years, the harm done to such seaboard towns as Tangier, Rabatand Casablanca is hard to estimate. The modern European colonistapparently imagined that to plant his warehouses, *cafés* andcinema-palaces within the walls which for so long had fiercely excludedhim was the most impressive way of proclaiming his domination.

Under General Lyautey such views are no longer tolerated. Respect fornative habits, native beliefs and native architecture is the firstprinciple inculcated in the civil servants attached to hisadministration. Not only does he require that the native towns shall bekept intact, and no European building erected within them; a sense ofbeauty not often vouchsafed to Colonial governors causes him to placethe administration buildings so far beyond the walls that the moderncolony grouped around them remains entirely distinct from the old town,instead of growing out of it like an ugly excrescence.

The Arab quarter of Rabat was already irreparably disfigured whenGeneral Lyautey came to Morocco; but ferocious old Salé, Pheniciancounting-house and breeder of Barbary pirates, had been saved fromprofanation by its Moslem fanaticism. Few Christian feet had entered itswalls except those of the prisoners who, like Robinson Crusoe, slavedfor the wealthy merchants in its mysterious terraced houses. Not tilltwo or three years ago was it completely pacified; and when it openedits gates to the infidel it was still, as it is to-day, the type of theuntouched Moroccan city—so untouched that, with the sunlightirradiating its cream-coloured walls and the blue-white domes abovethem, it rests on its carpet of rich fruit-gardens like some rarespecimen of Arab art on a strip of old Oriental velvet.

Within the walls, the magic persists: which does not always happen whenone penetrates into the mirage-like cities of Arabian Africa. Salé hasthe charm of extreme compactness. Crowded between the river-mouth andthe sea, its white and pale-blue houses almost touch across the narrowstreets, and the reed-thatched bazaars seem like miniature reductions ofthe great trading labyrinths of Tunis or Fez.

Everything that the reader of the Arabian Nights expects to find ishere: the whitewashed niches wherein pale youths sit weaving the finemattings for which the town is still famous; the tunnelled passageswhere indolent merchants with bare feet crouch in their little kennelshung with richly ornamented saddlery and arms, or with slippers of palecitron leather and bright embroidered *babouches*; the stalls withfruit, olives, tunny-fish, vague syrupy sweets, candles for saints'tombs, Mantegnesque garlands of red and green peppers, griddle-cakessizzling on red-hot pans, and all the varied wares and cakes andcondiments that the lady in the tale of the Three Calanders went out tobuy, that memorable morning in the market of Bagdad.

Only at Salé all is on a small scale: there is not much of any onething, except of the exquisite matting. The tide of commerce has ebbedfrom the intractable old city, and one feels, as one watches thelistless purchasers in her little languishing bazaars, that her longanimosity against the intruder has ended by destroying her own life.

The feeling increases when one leaves the bazaar for the streetsadjoining it. An even deeper hush than that which hangs over thewell-to-do quarters of all Arab towns broods over these silentthorough-fares, with heavy-nailed doors barring half-ruined houses. In asteep deserted square one of these doors opens its panels ofweather-silvered cedar on the court of the frailest, ghostliest ofMedersas—mere carved and painted shell of a dead house of learning.Mystic interweavings of endless lines, patient patterns interminablyrepeated in wood and stone and clay, all are here, from the tessellatedpaving of the court to the honeycombing of the cedar roof through whicha patch of sky shows here and there like an inset of turquoise tiling.

This lovely ruin is in the safe hands of the French Fine Artsadministration, and soon the wood-carvers and stucco-workers of Fez willhave revived its old perfection; but it will never again be more than ashow-Medersa, standing empty and unused beside the mosque behind whoseguarded doors and high walls one guesses that the old religiousfanaticism of Salé is dying also, as her learning and her commerce havedied.

In truth the only life in her is centred in the market-place outside the walls, where big expanding Rabat goes on certain days to provision herself. The market of Salé, though typical of all Moroccan markets, has an animation and picturesqueness of its own. Its rows of white tents pitched on a dusty square between the outer walls and the fruit-gardens make it look as though a hostile tribe had sat down to lay siege to the town; but the army is an army of hucksters, of farmers from the rich black lands along the river, of swarthy nomads and leather-gaitered peasant women from the hills, of slaves and servants and tradesmen from Rabat and Salé; a draped, veiled, turbaned mob shrieking, bargaining, fist-shaking, call on Allah to witness the monstrous villanies of the misbegotten miscreants they are trading with, and then, struck with the mysterious Eastern apathy, sinking down in languid heaps of muslin among the black figs, purple onions and rosy melons, the fluttering hens, the tethered goats, the whinnying foals, that are all enclosed in an outer circle of folded-up camels and of mules dozing under faded crimson saddles.

VI

CHELLA AND THE GREAT MOSQUE

The Merinid Sultans of Rabat had a terribly troublesome neighbour across the Bou-Regreg, and they built Chella to keep an eye on the pirates of Salé. But Chella has fallen like a Babylonian city triumphed over by the prophets; while Salé, sly, fierce and irrepressible, continued till well on in the nineteenth century to breed pirates and fanatics.

The ruins of Chella lie on the farther side of the plateau above the native town of Rabat. The mighty wall enclosing them faces the city wall of Rabat, looking at it across one of those great red powdery wastes which seem, in this strange land, like death and the desert forever creeping up to overwhelm the puny works of man.

The red waste is scored by countless trains of donkeys carrying water from the springs of Chella, by long caravans of mules and camels, and by the busy motors of the French administration; yet there emanates from it an impression of solitude and decay which even the prosaic tinkle of the trams jogging out from the European town to the Exhibition grounds above the sea cannot long dispel.

Perpetually, even in the new thriving French Morocco, the outline of aruin or the look in a pair of eyes shifts the scene, rends the thin veilof the European Illusion, and confronts one with the old grey Moslemreality. Passing under the gate of Chella, with its richly carvedcorbels and lofty crenellated towers, one feels one's self thuscompletely reabsorbed into the past.

Below the gate the ground slopes away, bare and blazing, to a hollowwhere a little blue-green minaret gleams through fig-trees, andfragments of arch and vaulting reveal the outline of a ruined mosque.

Was ever shade so blue-black and delicious as that of the cork-tree nearthe spring where the donkey's water-cans are being filled? Under itsbranches a black man in a blue shirt lies immovably sleeping in thedust. Close by women and children splash and chatter about the spring,and the dome of a saint's tomb shines through lustreless leaves. Theblack man, the donkeys, the women and children, the saint's dome, areall part of the inimitable Eastern scene in which inertia and agitationare so curiously combined, and a surface of shrill noise flickers overdepths of such unfathomable silence.

The ruins of Chella belong to the purest period of Moroccan art. Thetracery of the broken arches is all carved in stone or in glazedturquoise tiling, and the fragments of wall and vaulting have the firmelegance of a classic ruin. But what would even their beauty be withoutthe leafy setting of the place? The "unimaginable touch of Time" givesChella its peculiar charm: the aged fig-tree clamped in uptorn tiles andthrusting gouty arms between the arches; the garlanding of vines flungfrom column to column; the secret pool to which childless women arebrought to bathe, and where the tree springing from a cleft of the stepsis always hung with the bright bits of stuff which are the votiveofferings of Africa.

The shade, the sound of springs, the terraced orange-garden with irisesblooming along channels of running water, all this greenery and coolnessin the hollow of a fierce red hill make Chella seem, to the travellernew to Africa, the very type and embodiment of its old contrasts of heatand freshness, of fire and languor. It is like a desert traveller'sdream in his last fever.

Yacoub-el-Mansour was the fourth of the great Almohad Sultans who, inthe twelfth century, drove out the effete Almoravids, and swept theirvictorious armies from Marrakech to Tunis and from Tangier to

Madrid.His grandfather, Abd-el-Moumen, had been occupied with conquest andcivic administration. It was said of his rule that "he seized northernAfrica to make order prevail there"; and in fact, out of a welter ofwild tribes confusedly fighting and robbing he drew an empire firmlyseated and securely governed, wherein caravans travelled from the Atlasto the Straits without fear of attack, and "a soldier wandering throughthe fields would not have dared to pluck an ear of wheat."

His grandson, the great El-Mansour, was a conqueror too; but where heconquered he planted the undying seed of beauty. The victor of Alarcos,the soldier who subdued the north of Spain, dreamed a great dream ofart. His ambition was to bestow on his three capitals, Seville, Rabatand Marrakech, the three most beautiful towers the world had ever seen;and if the tower of Rabat had been completed, and that of Seville hadnot been injured by Spanish embellishments, his dream would have beenrealized.

The "Tower of Hassan," as the Sultan's tower is called, rises from theplateau above old Rabat, overlooking the steep cliff that drops down tothe last winding of the Bou-Regreg. Truncated at half its height, itstands on the edge of the cliff, a far-off beacon to travellers by landand sea. It is one of the world's great monuments, so sufficient instrength and majesty that until one has seen its fellow, the Koutoubyaof Marrakech, one wonders if the genius of the builder could havecarried such perfect balance of massive wall-spaces and traceriedopenings to a triumphant completion.

Near the tower, the red-brown walls and huge piers of the mosque builtat the same time stretch their roofless alignment beneath the sky. Thismosque, before it was destroyed, must have been one of the finestmonuments of Almohad architecture in Morocco: now, with its tumbled redmasses of masonry and vast cisterns overhung by clumps of blue aloes, itstill forms a ruin of Roman grandeur.

The Mosque, the Tower, the citadel of the Oudayas, and the mighty wallsand towers of Chella, compose an architectural group as noble andcomplete as that of some mediæval Tuscan city. All they need to make thecomparison exact is that they should have been compactly massed on asteep hill, instead of lying scattered over the wide spaces between thepromontory of the Oudayas and the hillside of Chella.

The founder of Rabat, the great Yacoub-el-Mansour, called it, in memory of the battle of Alarcos, "The Camp of Victory" (*Ribat-el-Path*), and the monuments he bestowed on it justified the name in another sense, by giving it the beauty that lives when battles are forgotten.

II
VOLUBILIS, MOULAY IDRISS AND MEKNEZ

I

VOLUBILIS

One day before sunrise we set out from Rabat for the ruins of RomanVolubilis.

From the ferry of the Bou-Regreg we looked backward on a last vision oforange ramparts under a night-blue sky sprinkled with stars; ahead, overgardens still deep in shadow, the walls of Salé were passing from drabto peach-colour in the eastern glow. Dawn is the romantic hour inAfrica. Dirt and dilapidation disappear under a pearly haze, and abreeze from the sea blows away the memory of fetid markets and sordidheaps of humanity. At that hour the old Moroccan cities look like theivory citadels in a Persian miniature, and the fat shopkeepers ridingout to their vegetable-gardens like Princes sallying forth to rescuecaptive maidens.

Our way led along the highroad from Rabat to the modern port of Kenitra,near the ruins of the Phenician colony of Mehedyia. Just north ofKenitra we struck the trail, branching off eastward to a Europeanvillage on the light railway between Rabat and Fez, and beyond therailway-sheds and flat-roofed stores the wilderness began, stretchingaway into clear distances bounded by the hills of the Rarb, abovewhich the sun was rising.

Range after range these translucent hills rose before us; all around thesolitude was complete. Village life, and even tent life, naturallygathers about a river-bank or a spring; and the waste we were crossingwas of waterless sand bound together by a loose desert growth. Only anabandoned well-curb here and there cast its blue shadow on the yellow*bled*, or a saint's tomb hung like a bubble between sky and sand. Thelight had the preternatural purity which gives a foretaste of mirage: itwas the light in which magic becomes real, and which helps to understandhow, to people living in such an atmosphere, the boundary between factand dream perpetually fluctuates.

The sand was scored with tracks and ruts innumerable, for the roadbetween Rabat and Fez is travelled not only by French government motorsbut by native caravans and trains of pilgrims to and from the sacredcity of Moulay Idriss, the founder of the Idrissite dynasty, whose tombis in the Zerhoun, the mountain ridge above Volubilis. To untrained eyesit was impossible to guess which of the trails one ought to follow; andwithout much surprise we suddenly found the motor stopping, while itswheels spun round vainly in the loose sand.

The military chauffeur was not surprised either; nor was Captain de M.,the French staff-officer who accompanied us.

"It often happens just here," they admitted philosophically. "When theGeneral goes to Meknez he is always followed by a number of motors, sothat if his own is stuck he may go on in another."

This was interesting to know, but not particularly helpful, as theGeneral and his motors were not travelling our way that morning. Nor wasany one else, apparently. It is curious how quickly the *bled* emptiesitself to the horizon if one happens to have an accident in it! But wehad learned our lesson between Tangier and Rabat, and were able toproduce a fair imitation of the fatalistic smile of the country.

The officer remarked cheerfully that somebody might turn up, and we allsat down in the *bled*.

A Berber woman, cropping up from nowhere, came and sat beside us. Shehad the thin sun-tanned face of her kind, brilliant eyes touched withkhol, high cheek-bones, and the exceedingly short upper lip whichgives such charm to the smile of the young nomad women. Her dress wasthe usual faded cotton shift, hooked on the shoulders with brass orsilver clasps (still the antique *fibulæ*), and wound about with a vaguedrapery in whose folds a brown baby wriggled.

The coolness of dawn had vanished and the sun beat down from a fiercesky. The village on the railway was too far off to be reached on foot,and there were probably no mules there to spare. Nearer at hand therewas no sign of help: not a fortified farm, or even a circle of nomadtents. It was the unadulterated desert—and we waited.

Not in vain; for after an hour or two, from far off in the direction ofthe hills, there appeared an army with banners. We stared at itunbelievingly. The *mirage*, of course! We were too sophisticated to doubt it, and tales of sun-dazed travellers mocked by such visions rose in our well-stocked memories.

The chauffeur thought otherwise. "Good! That's a pilgrimage from the mountains. They're going to Salé to pray at the tomb of the *marabout*; to-day is his feast-day."

And so they were! And as we hung on their approach, and speculated as to the chances of their stopping to help, I had time to note the beauty of this long train winding toward us under parti-colored banners. There was something celestial, almost diaphanous, in the hundreds of figures turbaned and draped in white, marching slowly through the hot colorless radiance over the hot colorless sand.

The most part were on foot, or bestriding tiny donkeys, but a stately Caïd rode alone at the end of the line on a horse saddled with crimson velvet; and to him our officer appealed.

The Caïd courteously responded, and twenty or thirty pilgrims were ordered to harness themselves to the motor and haul it back to the trail, while the rest of the procession moved hieratically onward.

I felt scruples at turning from their path even a fraction of this pious company; but they fell to with a saintly readiness, and before long the motor was on the trail. Then rewards were dispensed; and instantly those holy men became a prey to the darkest passions. Even in this land of contrasts the transition from pious serenity to rapacious rage can seldom have been more rapid. The devotees of the *marabout* fought, screamed, tore their garments and rolled over each other with sanguinary gestures in the struggle for our pesetas; then, perceiving our indifference, they suddenly remembered their religious duties, scrambled to their feet, tucked up their flying draperies, and raced after the tail-end of the procession.

Through a golden heat-haze we struggled on to the hills. The country was fallow, and in great part too sandy for agriculture; but here and there we came on one of the deep-set Moroccan rivers, with a reddish-yellow course channelled between perpendicular banks of red earth, and marked by a thin line of verdure that widened to fruit-gardens wherever a village had sprung up. We traversed several of these "sedentary" villages, *nourwals* of clay houses with thatched conical roofs, ingardens of fig, apricot and pomegranate that must be so many pink andwhite paradises after the winter rains.

One of these villages seemed to be inhabited entirely by blacks, bigfriendly creatures who came out to tell us by which trail to reach thebridge over the yellow *oued*. In the *oued* their womenkind werewashing the variegated family rags. They were handsome blue-bronzecreatures, bare to the waist, with tight black astrakhan curls andfirmly sculptured legs and ankles; and all around them, like a swarm ofgnats, danced countless jolly pickaninnies, naked as lizards, with thespindle legs and globular stomachs of children fed only on cereals.

Half terrified but wholly interested, these infants buzzed about themotor while we stopped to photograph them; and as we watched theirantics we wondered whether they were the descendants of the littleSoudanese boys whom the founder of Meknez, the terrible SultanMoulay-Ismaël, used to carry off from beyond the Atlas and bring up inhis military camps to form the nucleus of the Black Guard which defendedhis frontiers. We were on the line of travel between Meknez and the sea,and it seemed not unlikely that these *nourwals* were all that remainedof scattered outposts of Moulay-Ismaël's legionaries.

After a time we left *oueds* and villages behind us and were in themountains of the Rarb, toiling across a high sandy plateau. Far off afringe of vegetation showed promise of shade and water, and at last,against a pale mass of olive-trees, we saw the sight which, at whateverend of the world one comes upon it, wakes the same sense of awe: theruin of a Roman city.

Volubilis (called by the Arabs the Castle of the Pharaohs) is the onlyconsiderable Roman colony so far discovered in Morocco. It stands on theextreme ledge of a high plateau backed by the mountains of the Zerhoun.Below the plateau, the land drops down precipitately to a narrowriver-valley green with orchards and gardens, and in the neck of thevalley, where the hills meet again, the conical white town of MoulayIdriss, the Sacred City of Morocco, rises sharply against a woodedbackground.

So the two dominations look at each other across the valley: one, thelifeless Roman ruin, representing a system, an order, a socialconception that still run through all our modern ways; the other, theuntouched Moslem city, more dead and sucked back into an unintelligiblepast than any broken architrave of Greece or Rome.

Volubilis seems to have had the extent and wealth of a great militaryoutpost, such as Timgad in Algeria; but in the seventeenth century itwas very nearly destroyed by Moulay-Ismaël, the Sultan of the BlackGuard, who carried off its monuments piece-meal to build his new capitalof Meknez, that Mequinez of contemporary travellers which was held to beone of the wonders of the age.

Little remains to Volubilis in the way of important monuments: only thefragments of a basilica, part of an arch of triumph erected in honour ofCaracalla, and the fallen columns and architraves which strew the pathof Rome across the world. But its site is magnificent; and as theexcavation of the ruins was interrupted by the war it is possible thatsubsequent search may bring forth other treasures comparable to thebeautiful bronze *sloughi* (the African hound) which is now itsprincipal possession.

It was delicious, after seven hours of travel under the African sun, tosit on the shady terrace where the Curator of Volubilis, M. LouisChâtelain, welcomes his visitors. The French Fine Arts have built acharming house with gardens and pergolas for the custodian of the ruins,and have found in M. Châtelain an archæologist so absorbed in his taskthat, as soon as conditions permit, every inch of soil in thecircumference of the city will be made to yield up whatever secrets ithides.

II

MOULAY IDRISS

We lingered under the pergolas of Volubilis till the heat grew lessintolerable, and then our companions suggested a visit to Moulay Idriss.

Such a possibility had not occurred to us, and even Captain de M. seemedto doubt whether the expedition were advisable. Moulay Idriss was stillsaid to be resentful of Christian intrusion: it was only a year beforethat the first French officers had entered it.

But M. Châtelain was confident that there would be no opposition to ourvisit, and with the piled-up terraces and towers of the Sacred Citygrowing golden in the afternoon light across the valley it wasimpossible to hesitate.

We drove down through an olive-wood as ancient as those of Mitylene andCorfu, and then along the narrowing valley, between gardens luxurianteven in the parched Moroccan autumn. Presently the motor began to climbthe steep road to the town, and at a gateway we got out and were met bythe native chief of police. Instantly at the high windows of mysterioushouses veiled heads appeared and sidelong eyes cautiously inspected us.But the quarter was deserted, and we walked on without meeting any oneto the Street of the Weavers, a silent narrow way between lowwhitewashed niches like the cubicles in a convent. In each niche sat agrave white-robed youth, forming a great amphora-shaped grain-basket outof closely plaited straw. Vine-leaves and tendrils hung through the reedroofing overhead, and grape-clusters cast their classic shadow at ourfeet. It was like walking on the unrolled frieze of a white Etruscanvase patterned with black vine garlands.

The silence and emptiness of the place began to strike us: there was nosign of the Oriental crowd that usually springs out of the dust at theapproach of strangers. But suddenly we heard close by the lament of the*rekka* (a kind of long fife), accompanied by a wild thrum-thrum ofearthenware drums and a curious excited chanting of men's voices. I hadheard such a chant before, at the other end of North Africa, inKairouan, one of the other great Sanctuaries of Islam, where the sect ofthe Aïssaouas celebrate their sanguinary rites in the *Zaouïa* oftheir confraternity. Yet it seemed incredible that if the Aïssaouas ofMoulay Idriss were performing their ceremonies that day the chief ofpolice should be placidly leading us through the streets in the verydirection from which the chant was coming. The Moroccan, though he hasno desire to get into trouble with the Christian, prefers to be leftalone on feast-days, especially in such a stronghold of the faith asMoulay Idriss.

But "Geschehen ist geschehen" is the sum of Oriental philosophy. Forcenturies Moulay Idriss had held out fanatically on its holy steep;then, suddenly, in 1916, its chiefs saw that the game was up, andsurrendered without a pretense of resistance. Now the whole thing wasover, the new conditions were accepted, and the chief of police assuredus that with the French uniform at our side we should be safe anywhere.

"The Aïssaouas?" he explained. "No, this is another sect, the Hamadchas,who are performing their ritual dance on the feast-day of their patron,the *marabout* Hamadch, whose tomb is in the Zerhoun. The feast iscelebrated publicly in the market-place of Moulay Idriss."

As he spoke we came out into the market-place, and understood why therehad been no crowd at the gate. All the population was in the square andon the roofs that mount above it, tier by tier, against the woodedhillside: Moulay Idriss had better to do that day than to gape at a fewtourists in dust-coats.

Short of Sfax, and the other coast cities of eastern Tunisia, there issurely not another town in North Africa as white as Moulay Idriss. Someare pale blue and pinky yellow, like the Kasbah of Tangier, or cream andblue like Salé; but Tangier and Salé, for centuries continuouslysubject to European influences, have probably borrowed their colors fromGenoa and the Italian Riviera. In the interior of the country, andespecially in Morocco, where the whole color-scheme is much soberer thanin Algeria and Tunisia, the color of the native houses is always apenitential shade of mud and ashes.

But Moulay Idriss, that afternoon, was as white as if its arcaded squarehad been scooped out of a big cream cheese. The late sunlight lay likegold-leaf on one side of the square, the other was in pure blue shade;and above it, the crowded roofs, terraces and balconies packed withwomen in bright dresses looked like a flower-field on the edge of amarble quarry.

The bright dresses were as unusual a sight as the white walls, for theaverage Moroccan crowd is the color of its houses. But the occasion wasa special one, for these feasts of the Hamadchas occur only twice ayear, in spring and autumn, and as the ritual dances take place out ofdoors, instead of being performed inside the building of theconfraternity, the feminine population seizes the opportunity to burstinto flower on the house-tops.

It is rare, in Morocco, to see in the streets or the bazaars any womenexcept of the humblest classes, household slaves, servants, peasantsfrom the country or small tradesmen's wives; and even they (with theexception of the unveiled Berber women) are wrapped in the prevailinggrave-clothes. The *filles de joie* and dancing-girls whose brilliantdresses enliven certain streets of the Algerian and Tunisian towns areinvisible, or at least unnoticeable, in Morocco, where life, on thewhole, seems so much less gay and brightly-tinted; and the women of thericher classes, mercantile or aristocratic, never leave their haremsexcept to be married or buried. A throng of women dressed in lightcolors is therefore to be seen in public only when some street festivaldraws them to the roofs. Even then it is probable that the throng ismostly composed of slaves, household servants, and women of the lower*bourgeoisie*; but as they are all dressed in mauve and rose and palegreen, with long earrings and jewelled head-bands flashing through theirparted veils, the illusion, from a little distance, is as complete asthough they were the ladies in waiting of the Queen of Sheba; and thatradiant afternoon at Moulay Idriss, above the vine-garlanded square, andagainst the background of piled-up terraces, their vivid groups were insuch contrast to the usual gray assemblages of the East that the sceneseemed like a setting for some extravagantly staged ballet.

For the same reason the spectacle unrolling itself below us took on ablessed air of unreality. Any normal person who has seen a dance of theAïssaouas and watched them swallow thorns and hot coals, slashthemselves with knives, and roll on the floor in epilepsy must haveprivately longed, after the first excitement was over, to fly from therepulsive scene. The Hamadchas are much more savage than Aïssaouas, andcarry much farther their display of cataleptic anæsthesia; and, knowingthis, I had wondered how long I should be able to stand the sight ofwhat was going on below our terrace. But the beauty of the settingredeemed the bestial horror. In that unreal golden light the scenebecame merely symbolical: it was like one of those strange animal maskswhich the Middle Ages brought down from antiquity by way of thesatyr-plays of Greece, and of which the half-human protagonists stillgrin and contort themselves among the Christian symbols of Gothiccathedrals.

At one end of the square the musicians stood on a stone platform abovethe dancers. Like the musicians in a bas-relief they were flattenedside by side against a wall, the fife-players with lifted arms andinflated cheeks, the drummers pounding frantically on long earthenwaredrums shaped like enormous hour-glasses and painted in barbaricpatterns; and below, down the length of the market-place, the danceunrolled itself in a frenzied order that would have filled with envy aParis or London impresario.

In its centre an inspired-looking creature whirled about on his axis,the black ringlets standing out in snaky spirals from his haggard head,his cheek-muscles convulsively twitching. Around him, but a long wayoff, the dancers rocked and circled with long raucous cries dominated bythe sobbing booming music; and in the sunlit space between dancers andholy man, two or three impish children bobbed about with fixed eyes and a grimace of comic frenzy, solemnly parodying his contortions.

Meanwhile a tall grave personage in a doge-like cap, the only calm figure in the tumult, moved gravely here and there, regulating the dance, stimulating the frenzy, or calming some devotee who had broken the ranks and lay tossing and foaming on the stones. There was something far more sinister in this passionless figure, holding his hand on the key that let loose such crazy forces, than in the poor central whirligig who merely set the rhythm of the convulsions.

The dancers were all dressed in white caftans or in the blue shirts of the lowest classes. In the sunlight something that looked like fresh red paint glistened on their shaved black or yellow skulls and made dark blotches on their garments. At first these stripes and stains suggested only a gaudy ritual ornament like the pattern on the drums; then one saw that the paint, or whatever it was, kept dripping down from the whirling caftans and forming fresh pools among the stones; that as one of the pools dried up another formed, redder and more glistening, and that these pools were fed from great gashes which the dancers hacked in their own skulls and breasts with hatchets and sharpened stones. The dance was a blood-rite, a great sacrificial symbol, in which blood flowed so freely that all the rocking feet were splashed with it.

Gradually, however, it became evident that many of the dancers simply rocked and howled, without hacking themselves, and that most of the bleeding skulls and breasts belonged to negroes. Every now and then the circle widened to let in another figure, black or dark yellow, the figure of some humble blue-shirted spectator suddenly "getting religion" and rushing forward to snatch a weapon and baptize himself with his own blood; and as each new recruit joined the dancers the music shrieked louder and the devotees howled more wolfishly. And still, in the centre, the mad *marabout* spun, and the children bobbed and mimicked him and rolled their diamond eyes.

Such is the dance of the Hamadchas, of the confraternity of the *marabout* Hamadch, a powerful saint of the seventeenth century, whose tomb is in the Zerhoun above Moulay Idriss. Hamadch, it appears, had a faithful slave, who, when his master died, killed himself in despair, and the self-inflicted wounds of the brotherhood are supposed to symbolize the slave's suicide; though no doubt the origin of theceremony might be traced back to the depths of that ensanguined grovewhere Mr. Fraser plucked the Golden Bough.

The more naïve interpretation, however, has its advantages, since itenables the devotees to divide their ritual duties into two classes, thedevotions of the free men being addressed to the saint who died in hisbed, while the slaves belong to the slave, and must therefore simulatehis horrid end. And this is the reason why most of the white caftanssimply rock and writhe, while the humble blue shirts drip with blood.

The sun was setting when we came down from our terrace above themarket-place. To find a lodging for the night we had to press on toMeknez, where we were awaited at the French military post; therefore wewere reluctantly obliged to refuse an invitation to take tea with theCaïd, whose high-perched house commands the whole white amphitheatre ofthe town. It was disappointing to leave Moulay Idriss with the Hamadchashowling their maddest, and so much besides to see; but as we drove awayunder the long shadows of the olives we counted ourselves lucky to haveentered the sacred town, and luckier still to have been there on the dayof the dance which, till a year ago, no foreigner had been allowed tosee.

A fine French road runs from Moulay Idriss to Meknez, and we flew onthrough the dusk between wooded hills and open stretches on which thefires of nomad camps put orange splashes in the darkness. Then the moonrose, and by its light we saw a widening valley, and gardens andorchards that stretched up to a great walled city outlined against thestars.

III

MEKNEZ

All that evening, from the garden of the Military Subdivision on theopposite height, we sat and looked across at the dark tree-clumps andmoon-lit walls of Meknez, and listened to its fantastic history.

Meknez was built by the Sultan Moulay-Ismaël, around the nucleus of asmall town of which the site happened to please him, at the very momentwhen Louis XIV was creating Versailles. The coincidence of twocontemporary autocrats calling cities out of the wilderness has causedpersons with a taste for analogy to describe Meknez as the Versailles ofMorocco: an epithet which is about as instructive as it would be to callPhidias the Benvenuto Cellini of Greece.

There is, however, a pretext for the comparison in the fact that the twosovereigns took a lively interest in each other's affairs. Moulay-Ismaëlsent several embassies to treat with Louis XIV on the eternal questionof piracy and the ransom of Christian captives, and the two rulers werecontinually exchanging gifts and compliments.

The governor of Tetouan, who was sent to Paris in 1680, having broughtas presents to the French King a lion, a lioness, a tigress, and fourostriches, Louis XIV shortly afterward despatched M. de Saint-Amand toMorocco with two dozen watches, twelve pieces of gold brocade, a cannonsix feet long and other firearms. After this the relations between thetwo courts remained friendly till 1693, at which time they were strainedby the refusal of France to return the Moorish captives who wereemployed on the king's galleys, and who were probably as much neededthere as the Sultan's Christian slaves for the building of Moorishpalaces.

Six years later the Sultan despatched Abdallah-ben-Aïssa to France toreopen negotiations. The ambassador was as brilliantly received and aseagerly run after as a modern statesman on an official mission, and hiscandidly expressed admiration for the personal charms of the Princessede Conti, one of the French monarch's legitimatized children, issupposed to have been mistaken by the court for an offer of marriagefrom the Emperor of Barbary. But he came back without a treaty.

Moulay-Ismaël, whose long reign (1673 to 1727) and extraordinaryexploits make him already a legendary figure, conceived, early in hiscareer, a passion for Meknez; and through all his troubled rule, withits alternations of barbaric warfare and far-reaching negotiations,palace intrigue, crazy bloodshed and great administrative reforms, hisheart perpetually reverted to the wooded slopes on which he dreamed ofbuilding a city more splendid than Fez or Marrakech.

"The Sultan" (writes his chronicler Aboul Kasim-ibn-Ahmad, called"Ezziani") "loved Meknez, the climate of which had enchanted him, and hewould have liked never to leave it." He left it, indeed, often, left itperpetually, to fight with revolted tribes in the Atlas, to defeat oneBerber army after another, to carry his arms across the High Atlas intothe Souss, to adorn Fez with the heads of seven hundred vanquishedchiefs, to put down his three rebellious brothers, to strip all thecities of his empire of their negroes and transport them to Meknez ("sothat not a negro, man, woman or child, slave or free, was left in anypart of the country"); to fight and defeat the Christians (1683); totake Tangier, to conduct a campaign on the Moulouya, to lead the holywar against the Spanish (1689), to take Larache, the Spanish commercialpost on the west coast (which furnished eighteen hundred captives forMeknez); to lay siege to Ceuta, conduct a campaign against the Turks ofAlgiers, repress the pillage in his army, subdue more tribes, and buildforts for his Black Legionaries from Oudjda to the Oued Noun. But almosteach year's bloody record ends with the placid phrase: "Then the Sultanreturned to Meknez."

In the year 1701, Ezziani writes, the indomitable old man "deprived hisrebellious sons of their principalities; after which date he consecratedhimself exclusively to the building of his palaces and the planting ofhis gardens. And in 1720 (nineteen years later in this long reign!) heordered the destruction of the mausoleum of Moulay Idriss for thepurpose of enlarging it. And to gain the necessary space he bought allthe adjacent land, and the workmen did not leave these new labors tillthey were entirely completed."

In this same year there was levied on Fez a new tax which was so heavythat the inhabitants were obliged to abandon the city.

Yet it is written of this terrible old monarch, who devastated wholedistricts, and sacrificed uncounted thousands of lives for his ruthlesspleasure, that under his administration of his chaotic and turbulentempire "the country rejoiced in the most complete security. A Jew or awoman might travel alone from Oudjda to the Oued Noun without any one'sasking their business. Abundance reigned throughout the land: grain,food, cattle were to be bought for the lowest prices. Nowhere in thewhole of Morocco was a highwayman or a robber to be found."

And probably both sides of the picture are true.

*　　*　　*　　*　　*

What, then, was the marvel across the valley, what were the "lordlypleasure-houses" to whose creation and enlargement

Moulay-Ismaël returned again and again amid the throes and violences of a nearly centenarian life?

The chronicler continues: "The Sultan caused all the houses near the Kasbah to be demolished, *and compelled the inhabitants to carry away the ruins of their dwellings.* All the eastern end of the town was also torn down, and the ramparts were rebuilt. He also built the Great Mosque next to the palace of Nasr.... He occupied himself personally with the construction of his palaces, and before one was finished he caused another to be begun. He built the mosque of Elakhdar; the walls of the new town were pierced with twenty fortified gates and surmounted with platforms for cannon. Within the walls he made a great artificial lake where one might row in boats. There was also a granary with immense subterranean reservoirs of water, and a stable *three miles long* for the Sultan's horses and mules; twelve thousand horses could be stabled in it. The flooring rested on vaults in which the grain for the horses was stored.... He also built the palace of Elmansour, which had twenty cupolas; from the top of each cupola one could look forth on the plain and the mountains around Meknez. All about the stables the rarest trees were planted. Within the walls were fifty palaces, each with its own mosque and its baths. Never was such a thing known in any country, Arab or foreign, pagan or Moslem. The guarding of the doors of these palaces was intrusted to twelve hundred black eunuchs."

Such were the wonders that seventeenth century travellers toiled across the desert to see, and from which they came back dazzled and almost incredulous, as if half-suspecting that some djinn had deluded them with the vision of a phantom city. But for the soberer European records, and the evidence of the ruins themselves (for the whole of the new Meknez is a ruin), one might indeed be inclined to regard Ezziani's statements as an Oriental fable; but the briefest glimpse of Moulay-Ismaël's Meknez makes it easy to believe all his chronicler tells of it, even to the three miles of stables.

Next morning we drove across the valley and, skirting the old town on the hill, entered, by one of the twenty gates of Moulay-Ismaël, a long empty street lined with half-ruined arcades. Beyond was another street of beaten red earth bordered by high red walls blotched with gray and mauve. Ahead of us this road stretched out interminably (Meknez, before Washington, was the "city of magnificent distances"), and down its empty length only one or two draped figures passed, like shadows on the way toShadowland. It was clear that the living held no further traffic withthe Meknez of Moulay-Ismaël.

Here it was at last. Another great gateway let us, under a resplendentlybejewelled arch of turquoise-blue and green, into another walledemptiness of red clay; a third gate opened into still vaster vacancies,and at their farther end rose a colossal red ruin, something like thelower stories of a Roman amphitheatre that should stretch outindefinitely instead of forming a circle, or like a series of Romanaqueducts built side by side and joined into one structure. Below thisindescribable ruin the arid ground sloped down to an artificial waterwhich was surely the lake that the Sultan had made for hisboating-parties; and beyond it more red earth stretched away to morewalls and gates, with glimpses of abandoned palaces and huge crumblingangle-towers.

The vastness, the silence, the catastrophic desolation of the place,were all the more impressive because of the relatively recent date ofthe buildings. As Moulay-Ismaël had dealt with Volubilis, so time haddealt with his own Meknez; and the destruction which it had takenthousands of lash-driven slaves to inflict on the stout walls of theRoman city, neglect and abandonment had here rapidly accomplished. Butthough the sun-baked clay of which the impatient Sultan built hispleasure-houses will not suffer comparison with the firm stones of Rome,"the high Roman fashion" is visible in the shape and outline of theseruins. What they are no one knows. In spite of Ezziani's text (writtenwhen the place was already partly destroyed) archæologists disagree asto the uses of the crypt of rose-flushed clay whose twenty rows ofgigantic arches are so like an alignment of Roman aqueducts. Were thesethe vaulted granaries, or the subterranean reservoirs under the threemiles of stabling which housed the twelve thousand horses? The stables,at any rate, were certainly near this spot, for the lake adjoins theruins as in the chronicler's description; and between it and oldMeknez, behind walls within walls, lie all that remains of the fiftypalaces with their cupolas, gardens, mosques and baths.

This inner region is less ruined than the mysterious vaulted structure,and one of the palaces, being still reserved for the present Sultan'suse, cannot be visited; but we wandered unchallenged through desertcourts, gardens of cypress and olive where dried fountains and paintedsummer-houses are falling into dust, and barren spaces enclosed in longempty façades. It was all the work of an eager and imperious old man,who, to realize his dream quickly, built in perishable materials; butthe design, the dimensions, the whole conception, show that he had notonly heard of Versailles but had looked with his own eyes on Volubilis.

To build on such a scale, and finish the work in a single lifetime, evenif the materials be malleable and the life a long one, implies a commandof human labor that the other Sultan at Versailles must have envied.The imposition of the *corvée* was of course even simpler in Moroccothan in France, since the material to draw on was unlimited, providedone could assert one's power over it; and for that purpose Ismaël hadhis Black Army, the hundred and fifty thousand disciplined legionarieswho enabled him to enforce his rule over all the wild country fromAlgiers to Agadir.

The methods by which this army were raised and increased are worthrecounting in Ezziani's words:

"A *taleb* of Marrakech having shown the Sultan a register containingthe names of the negroes who had formed part of the army of El-Mansour,Moulay-Ismaël ordered his agents to collect all that remained of thesenegroes and their children.... He also sent to the tribes of theBeni-Hasen, and into the mountains, to purchase all the negroes to befound there. Thus all that were in the whole of Moghreb were assembled,from the cities and the countryside, till not one was left, slave orfree.

"These negroes were armed and clothed, and sent to Mechra Erremel (northof Meknez) where they were ordered to build themselves houses, plantgardens and remain till their children were ten years old. Then theSultan caused all the children to be brought to him, both boys andgirls. The boys were apprenticed to masons, carpenters, and othertradesmen; others were employed to make mortar. The next year they weretaught to drive the mules, the third to make *adobe* for building; thefourth year they learned to ride horses bareback, the fifth they weretaught to ride in the saddle while using firearms. At the age of sixteenthese boys became soldiers. They were then married to the youngnegresses who had meanwhile been taught cooking and washing in theSultan's palaces—except those who were pretty, and these were given amusical education, after which each one received a wedding-dress and amarriage settlement, and was handed over to her husband.

"All the children of these couples were in due time destined for theBlack Army, or for domestic service in the palaces. Every year theSultan went to the camp at Mechra Erremel and brought back thechildren. The Black Army numbered one hundred and fifty thousand men, ofwhom part were at Erremel, part at Meknez, and the rest in theseventy-six forts which the Sultan built for them throughout his domain.May the Lord be merciful to his memory!"

Such was the army by means of which Ismaël enforced the *corvée* on hisundisciplined tribes. Many thousands of lives went to the building ofimperial Meknez; but his subjects would scarcely have sufficed if he hadnot been able to add to them twenty-five thousand Christian captives.

M. Augustin Bernard, in his admirable book on Morocco, says that theseventeenth century was "the golden age of piracy" in Morocco; and thegreat Ismaël was no doubt one of its chief promoters. One understandshis unwillingness to come to an agreement with his great friend andcompetitor, Louis XIV, on the difficult subject of the ransom ofChristian captives when one reads in the admiring Ezziani that it tookfifty-five thousand prisoners and captives to execute his architecturalconceptions.

"These prisoners, by day, were occupied on various tasks; at night theywere locked into subterranean dungeons. Any prisoner who died at histask was *built into the wall he was building.*" (This statement isconfirmed by John Windus, the English traveller who visited the court ofMoulay-Ismaël in the Sultan's old age.) Many Europeans must havesuccumbed quickly to the heat and the lash, for the wall-builders wereobliged to make each stroke in time with their neighbors, and werebastinadoed mercilessly if they broke the rhythm; and there is littledoubt that the expert artisans of France, Italy and Spain were evendearer to the old architectural madman than the friendship of thepalace-building despot across the sea.

Ezziani's chronicle dates from the first part of the nineteenth century,and is an Arab's colorless panegyric of a great Arab ruler; but JohnWindus, the Englishman who accompanied Commodore Stewart's embassy toMeknez in 1721, saw the imperial palaces and their builder with his owneyes, and described them with the vivacity of a foreigner struck byevery contrast.

Moulay-Ismaël was then about eighty-seven years old, "a middle-sizedman, who has the remains of a good face, with nothing of a negro'sfeatures, though his mother was a black. He has a high nose, which ispretty long from the eye-brows downward, and thin. He has lost all histeeth, and breathes short, as if his lungs were bad, coughs and spitspretty often, which never falls to the ground, men being always readywith handkerchiefs to receive it. His beard is thin and very white, hiseyes seem to have been sparkling, but their vigor decayed through age,and his cheeks very much sunk in."

Such was the appearance of this extraordinary man, who deceived,tortured, betrayed, assassinated, terrorized and mocked his slaves, hissubjects, his women and children and his ministers like any otherhalf-savage Arab despot, but who yet managed through his long reign tomaintain a barbarous empire, to police the wilderness, and give at leastan appearance of prosperity and security where all had before beenchaos.

The English emissaries appear to have been much struck by themagnificence of his palaces, then in all the splendor of novelty, andgleaming with marbles brought from Volubilis and Salé. Windus extols inparticular the sunken gardens of cypress, pomegranate and orange trees,some of them laid out seventy feet below the level of the palace-courts;the exquisite plaster fretwork; the miles of tessellated walls andpavement made in the finely patterned mosaic work of Fez; and the longterrace walk trellised with "vines and other greens" leading from thepalace to the famous stables, and over which it was the Sultan's customto drive in a chariot drawn by women and eunuchs.

Moulay-Ismaël received the English ambassador with every show of pompand friendship, and immediately "made him a present" of a handful ofyoung English captives; but just as the negotiations were about to beconcluded Commodore Stewart was privately advised that the Sultan had nointention of allowing the rest of the English to be ransomed. Luckily adiplomatically composed letter, addressed by the English envoy to one ofthe favorite wives, resulted in Ismaël's changing his mind, and thecaptives were finally given up, and departed with their rescuers. As onestands in the fiery sun, among the monstrous ruins of those tragicwalls, one pictures the other Christian captives pausing for a second,at the risk of death, in the rhythmic beat of their labor, to watch thelittle train of their companions winding away across the desert tofreedom.

On the way back through the long streets that lead to the ruins wenoticed, lying by the roadside, the shafts of fluted columns, blocks ofmarble, Roman capitals: fragments of the long loot of Salé andVolubilis. We asked how they came there, and were told that, accordingto a tradition still believed in the country, when the prisoners andcaptives who were dragging the building materials toward the palaceunder the blistering sun heard of the old Sultan's death, they droppedtheir loads with one accord and fled. At the same moment every worker onthe walls flung down his trowel or hod, every slave of the palacesstopped grinding or scouring or drawing water or carrying faggots orpolishing the miles of tessellated floors; so that, when the tyrant'sheart stopped beating, at that very instant life ceased to circulate inthe huge house he had built, and in all its members it became a carcassfor his carcass.

III
FEZ

I

THE FIRST VISION

Many-walled Fez rose up before us out of the plain toward the end of theday.

The walls and towers we saw were those of the upper town, Fez Eldjid(the New), which lies on the edge of the plateau and hides from view OldFez tumbling down below it into the ravine of the Oued Fez. Thusapproached, the city presents to view only a long line of ramparts andfortresses, merging into the wide, tawny plain and framed in barrenmountains. Not a house is visible outside the walls, except, at arespectful distance, the few unobtrusive buildings of the Europeancolony; and not a village breaks the desolation of the landscape.

As we drew nearer, the walls towered close over us, and skirting them wecame to a bare space outside a great horseshoe gate, and found ourselvessuddenly in the foreground of a picture by Carpaccio or Bellini. Whereelse had one seen just those rows of white-turbaned majestic figures,squatting in the dust under lofty walls, all the pale faces ringed incurling beards turned to the story-teller in the centre of the group?Transform the story-teller into a rapt young Venetian, and you have theaudience and the foreground of Carpaccio's "Preaching of St. Stephen,"even to the camels craning inquisitive necks above the turbans. Everystep of the way in North Africa corroborates the close observation ofthe early travellers, whether painters or narrators, and shows theunchanged character of the Oriental life that the Venetians pictured,and Leo Africanus and Windus and Charles Cochelet described.

There was time, before sunset, to go up to the hill, from which theruined tombs of the Merinid Sultans look down over the city they madeglorious. After the savage massacre of foreign residents in 1912 theFrench encircled the heights commanding Fez with one of their admirablyengineered military roads, and in a few minutes our motor had climbed tothe point from which the great dynasty of artist-Sultans dreamed oflooking down forever on their capital.

Nothing endures in Islam, except what human inertia has left standingand its own solidity has preserved from the elements. Or rather, nothingremains intact, and nothing wholly perishes, but the architecture, likeall else, lingers on half-ruined and half-unchanged. The Merinid tombs,however, are only hollow shells and broken walls, grown part of thebrown cliff they cling to. No one thinks of them save as an added touchof picturesqueness where all is picturesque: they survive as the bestpoint from which to look down at Fez.

There it lies, outspread in golden light, roofs, terraces, and towerssliding over the plain's edge in a rush dammed here and there bybarriers of cypress and ilex, but growing more precipitous as theravine of the Fez narrows downward with the fall of the river. It is asthough some powerful enchanter, after decreeing that the city should behurled into the depths, had been moved by its beauty, and with a wave ofhis wand held it suspended above destruction.

At first the eye takes in only this impression of a great city over agreen abyss; then the complex scene begins to define itself. All aroundare the outer lines of ramparts, walls beyond walls, their crenellationsclimbing the heights, their angle fortresses dominating the precipices.Almost on a level with us lies the upper city, the aristocratic FezEldjid of painted palaces and gardens; then, as the houses close in anddescend more abruptly, terraces, minarets, domes, and long reed-thatchedroofs of the bazaars, all gather around the green-tiled tomb of MoulayIdriss, and the tower of the Almohad mosque of El Kairouiyin, whichadjoin each other in the depths of Fez, and form its central sanctuary.

*   *   *   *   *

From the Merinid hill we had noticed a long façade among the cypressesand fruit-trees of Eldjid. This was Bou-Jeloud, the old summer-palaceof the Sultan's harem, now the house of the Resident-General, wherelodgings had been prepared for us.

The road descended again, crossing the Oued Fez by one of the fine oldsingle-arch bridges that mark the architectural link between Morocco andSpain. We skirted high walls, wayside pools, and dripping mill-wheels;then one of the city gates engulfed us, and we were in the waste spacesof intramural Fez, formerly the lines of defense of a rich andperpetually menaced city, now chiefly used for refuse-heaps, open-airfondaks, and dreaming-places for rows of Lazaruses rolled in theircerements in the dust.

Through another gate and more walls we came to an arch in the inner lineof defense. Beyond that, the motor paused before a green door, where aCadi in a silken caftan received us. Across squares of orange-treesdivided by running water we were led to an arcaded apartment hung withMoroccan embroideries and lined with wide divans; the hall of receptionof the Resident-General. Through its arches were other tiled distances,fountains, arcades; beyond, in greener depths, the bright blossoms of aflower-garden. Such was our first sight of Bou-Jeloud, once thesummer-palace of the wives of Moulay Hafid.

Upstairs, from a room walled and ceiled with cedar, and decorated withthe bold rose-pink embroideries of Salé and the intricate old needleworkof Fez, I looked out over the upper city toward the mauve and tawnymountains.

Just below the window the flat roofs of a group of little housesdescended like the steps of an irregular staircase. Between them rose afew cypresses and a green minaret; out of the court of one house anancient fig-tree thrust its twisted arms. The sun had set, and one afteranother bright figures appeared on the roofs. The children came first,hung with silver amulets and amber beads, and pursued by negresses instriped turbans, who bustled up with rugs and matting; then the mothersfollowed more indolently, released from their ashy mufflings andshowing, under their light veils, long earrings from the *Mellah*and caftans of pale green or peach color.

The houses were humble ones, such as grow up in the cracks of a wealthyquarter, and their inhabitants doubtless small folk; but in theenchanted African twilight the terraces blossomed like gardens, and whenthe moon rose and the muezzin called from the minaret, the domesticsquabbles and the shrill cries from roof to roof became part of a storyin Bagdad, overheard a thousand years ago by that arch-detectiveHaroun-al-Raschid.

II

FEZ ELDJID

It is usual to speak of Fez as very old, and the term seems justifiedwhen one remembers that the palace of Bou-Jeloud stands on the site ofan Almoravid Kasbah of the eleventh century, that when that Kasbah waserected Fez Elbali had already existed for three hundred years, that ElKairouiyin is the contemporary of Sant' Ambrogio of Milan, and that theoriginal mosque of Moulay Idriss II was built over his grave in theeighth century.

Fez is, in fact, the oldest city in Morocco without a Phenician or aRoman past, and has preserved more traces than any other of itsarchitectural flowering-time; yet it would be truer to say of it, as ofall Moroccan cities, that it has no age, since its seemingly immutableshape is forever crumbling and being renewed on the old lines.

When we rode forth the next day to visit some of the palaces of Eldjidour pink-saddled mules carried us at once out of the bounds of time. Howassociate anything so precise and Occidental as years or centuries withthese visions offrail splendor seen through cypresses and roses? TheCadis in their multiple muslins, who received us in secret doorways andled us by many passages into the sudden wonder of gardens and fountains;the bright-earringed negresses peering down from painted balconies; thepilgrims and clients dozing in the sun against hot walls; the desertedhalls with plaster lace-work and gold pendentives in tiled niches; theVenetian chandeliers and tawdry rococo beds; the terraces from whichpigeons whirled up in a white cloud while we walked on a carpet of theirfeathers—were all these the ghosts of vanished state, or the actualsetting of the life of some rich merchant with "business connections"in Liverpool and Lyons, or some government official at that very momentspeeding to Meknez or Casablanca in his sixty h. p. motor?

We visited old palaces and new, inhabited and abandoned, and over alllay the same fine dust of oblivion, like the silvery mould on anoverripe fruit. Overripeness is indeed the characteristic of this richand stagnant civilization. Buildings, people, customs, seem all about tocrumble and fall of their own weight: the present is a perpetuallyprolonged past. To touch the past with one's hands is realized only indreams; and in Morocco the dream-feeling envelopes one at every step.One trembles continually lest the "Person from Porlock" should step in.

He is undoubtedly on the way; but Fez had not heard of him when we rodeout that morning. Fez Eldjid, the "New Fez" of palaces and governmentbuildings, was founded in the fourteenth century by the Merinid princes,and probably looks much as it did then. The palaces in their overgrowngardens, with pale-green trellises dividing the rose-beds from theblue-and-white tiled paths, and fountains in fluted basins of Italianmarble, all had the same drowsy charm; yet the oldest were built notmore than a century or two ago, others within the last fifty years; andat Marrakech, later in our journey, we were to visit a sumptuousdwelling where plaster-cutters and ceramists from Fez were actuallyrepeating with wonderful skill and spontaneity, the old ornamentation ofwhich the threads run back to Rome and Damascus.

Of really old private dwellings, palaces or rich men's houses, there aresurprisingly few in Morocco. It is hard to guess the age of some of thefeatureless houses propping each other's flanks in old Fez or old Salé;but people rich enough to rebuild have always done so, and the passionfor building seems allied, in this country of inconsequences, to thesupine indifference that lets existing constructions crumble back toclay. "Dust to dust" should have been the motto of the Moroccanpalace-builders.

Fez possesses one old secular building, a fine fondak of the fifteenthcentury; but in Morocco, as a rule, only mosques and the tombs of saintsare preserved—none too carefully—and even the strong stone buildingsof the Almohads have been allowed to fall to ruin, as at Chella andRabat. This indifference to the completed object—which is like a kindof collective exaggeration of the artist's indifference to his completedwork—has resulted in the total disappearance of the furniture and worksof art which must have filled the beautiful buildings of the Merinidperiod. Neither pottery nor brass-work nor enamels nor fine hangingssurvive; there is no parallel in Morocco to the textiles of Syria, thepotteries of Persia, the Byzantine ivories or enamels. It has been saidthat the Moroccan is always a nomad, who lives in his house as if itwere a tent; but this is not a conclusive answer to any one who knowsthe passion of the modern Moroccan for European furniture. When onereads the list of the treasures contained in the palaces of the ·

mediævalSultans of Egypt one feels sure that, if artists were lacking inMorocco, the princes and merchants who brought skilled craftsmen acrossthe desert to build their cities must also have imported treasures toadorn them. Yet, as far as is known, the famous fourteenth-centurybronze chandelier of Tetuan, and the fine old ritual furniture reportedto be contained in certain mosques, are the only important works of artin Morocco later in date than the Roman *sloughi* of Volubilis.

III

FEZ ELBALI

The distances in Fez are so great and the streets so narrow, and in somequarters so crowded, that all but saints or humble folk go about onmule-back.

In the afternoon, accordingly, the pink mules came again, and we set outfor the long tunnel-like street that leads down the hill to the FezElbali.

"Look out—'ware heads!" our leader would call back at every turn, asour way shrank to a black passage under a house bestriding the street,or a caravan of donkeys laden with obstructive reeds or branches ofdates made the passers-by flatten themselves against the walls.

On each side of the street the houses hung over us like fortresses,leaning across the narrow strip of blue and throwing out great beams andbuttresses to prop each other's bulging sides. Windows there were noneon the lower floors; only here and there an iron-barred slit stuffedwith rags and immemorial filth, from which a lean cat would suddenlyspring out, and scuttle off under an archway like a witch's familiar.

Some of these descending lanes were packed with people, others asdeserted as a cemetery; and it was strange to pass from the throngedstreets leading to the bazaars to the profound and secretive silence ofa quarter of well-to-do dwelling-houses, where only a few veiled womenattended by negro slaves moved noiselessly over the clean cobblestones,and the sound of fountains and runnels came from hidden courtyards andover garden-walls.

This noise of water is as characteristic of Fez as of Damascus. The OuedFez rushes through the heart of the town, bridged, canalized, builtover, and ever and again bursting out into tumultuous falls and poolsshadowed with foliage. The central artery of the city is not a streetbut a waterfall; and tales are told of the dark uses to which, evennow, the underground currents are put by some of the dwellers behind theblank walls and scented gardens of those highly respectable streets.

The crowd in Oriental cities is made up of many elements, and in MoroccoTurks, Jews and infidels, Berbers of the mountains, fanatics of theconfraternities, Soudanese blacks and haggard Blue Men of the Souss,jostle the merchants and government officials with that democraticfamiliarity which goes side by side with abject servility in this landof perpetual contradictions. But Fez is above all the city of wealth andlearning, of universities and counting-houses, and the merchant and the*oulama*—the sedentary and luxurious types—prevail.

The slippered Fazi merchant, wrapped in white muslins and securelymounted on a broad velvet saddle-cloth anchored to the back of a broadmule, is as unlike the Arab horseman of the desert as Mr. Tracy Tupmanwas unlike the Musketeers of Dumas. Ease, music, money-making, theaffairs of his harem and the bringing-up of his children, are his chiefinterests, and his plump pale face with long-lashed hazel eyes, hiscurling beard and fat womanish hands, recall the portly potentates ofHindu miniatures, dreaming among houris beside lotus-tanks.

These personages, when they ride abroad, are preceded by a swarthyfootman, who keeps his hand on the embroidered bridle; and thegovernment officers and dignitaries of the *Makhzen* are usuallyescorted by several mounted officers of their household, with a servantto each mule. The cry of the runners scatters the crowd, and even thepanniered donkeys and perpetually astonished camels somehow contrive tobecome two-dimensional while the white procession goes by.

Then the populace closes in again, so quickly and densely that it seemsimpossible it could ever have been parted, and negro water-carriers,muffled women, beggars streaming with sores, sinewy and greasy "saints,"Soudanese sorcerers hung with amulets made ofsardine-boxes andhares'-feet, long-lashed boys of the Chleuh in clean embroideredcaftans, Jews in black robes and skull-caps, university studentscarrying their prayer-carpets, bangled and spangled black women,scrofulous children with gazelle eyes and mangy skulls, and blind mentapping along with linked arms and howling out verses of the Koran,surge together in a mass drawn by irresistible suction to the pointwhere the bazaars converge about the mosques of Moulay Idriss and ElKairouiyin.

Seen from a terrace of the upper town, the long thatched roofing of ElAttarine, the central bazaar of Fez, promises fantastic revelations ofnative life; but the dun-colored crowds moving through its checkeredtwilight, the lack of carved shop-fronts and gaily adornedcoffee-houses, and the absence of the painted coffers and vividembroideries of Tunis, remind one that Morocco is a melancholy country,and Fez a profoundly melancholy city.

Dust and ashes, dust and ashes, echoes from the gray walls, themouldering thatch of the *souks*, the long lamentable song of the blindbeggars sitting in rows under the feet of the camels and asses. No youngmen stroll through the bazaar in bright caftans, with roses and jasminebehind their ears, no pedlars offer lemonade and sweetmeats and goldenfritters, no flower-sellers pursue one with tight bunches oforange-blossom and little pink roses. The well-to-do ride by in white,and the rest of the population goes mournfully in earth-color.

But gradually one falls under the spell of another influence—theinfluence of the Atlas and the desert. Unknown Africa seems much nearerto Morocco than to the white towns of Tunis and the smiling oases ofSouth Algeria. One feels the nearness of Marrakech at Fez, and atMarrakech that of Timbuctoo.

Fez is sombre, and the bazaars clustered about its holiest sanctuariesform its most sombre quarter. Dusk falls there early, and oil-lanternstwinkle in the merchants' niches while the clear African daylight stilllies on the gardens of upper Fez. This twilight adds to the mystery ofthe *souks*, making them, in spite of profane noise and crowding andfilth, an impressive approach to the sacred places.

Until a year or two ago, the precincts around Moulay Idriss and ElKairouiyin were *horm*, that is, cut off from the unbeliever. Heavybeams of wood barred the end of each *souk*, shutting off thesanctuaries, and the Christian could only conjecture what lay beyond.Now he knows in part; for, though the beams have not been lowered, allcomers may pass under them to the lanes about the mosques, and evenpause a moment in their open doorways. Farther one may not go, for theshrines of Morocco are still closed to unbelievers; but whoever knowsCordova, or has stood under the arches of the Great Mosque of Kairouan,can reconstruct something of the hidden beauties of its namesake, the"Mosque Kairouan" of western Africa.

Once under the bars, the richness of the old Moorish Fez presses uponone with unexpected beauty. Here is the graceful tiled fountain ofNedjarine, glittering with the unapproachable blues and greens ofceramic mosaics; near it, the courtyard of the Fondak Nedjarine, oldestand stateliest of Moroccan inns, with triple galleries of sculpturedcedar rising above arcades of stone. A little farther on lights andincense draw one to a threshold where it is well not to linger unduly.Under a deep archway, between booths where gay votive candles are sold,the glimmer of hanging lamps falls on patches of gilding and mosaic, andon veiled women prostrating themselves before an invisible shrine—forthis is the vestibule of the mosque of Moulay Idriss, where, on certaindays of the week, women are admitted to pray.

Moulay Idriss was not built over the grave of the Fatimite prophet,first of the name, whose bones lie in the Zerhoun above his sacred town.The mosque of Fez grew up around the tomb of his posthumous son, MoulayIdriss II, who, descending from the hills, fell upon a camp of Berberson an affluent of the Sebou, and there laid the foundations of Fez, andof the Moroccan Empire.

Of the original monument it is said that little remains. The*zaouïa* which encloses it dates from the reign of Moulay-Ismaël,the seventeenth-century Sultan of Meknez, and the mosque itself, and thegreen minaret shooting up from the very centre of old Fez, were notbuilt until 1820. But a rich surface of age has already formed on allthese disparate buildings, and the over-gorgeous details of the shrinesand fountains set in their outer walls are blended into harmony by afilm of incense-smoke, and the grease of countless venerating lips andhands.

Featureless walls of mean houses close in again at the next turn; but afew steps farther another archway reveals another secret scene. Thistime it is a corner of the jealously guarded court of ablutions in thegreat mosque El Kairouiyin, with the twin green-roofed pavilions thatare so like those of the Alhambra.

Those who have walked around the outer walls of the mosque of the otherKairouan, and recall the successive doors opening into the forecourt andinto the mosque itself, will be able to guess at the plan of the churchof Fez. The great Almohad sanctuary of Tunisia is singularly free fromparasitic buildings, and may be approached as easily as that of Cordova;but the approaches of El Kairouiyin are so built up that one never knowsat which turn of the labyrinth one may catch sight of its court offountains, or peep down the endless colonnades of which the Arabs say:"The man who should try to count the columns of Kairouiyin would gomad."

Marble floors, heavy whitewashed piers, prostrate figures in thepenumbra, rows of yellow slippers outside in the sunlight—out of suchglimpses one must reconstruct a vision of the long vistas of arches, theblues and golds of the *mirhab*, the lustre of bronze chandeliers,and the ivory inlaying of the twelfth-century *minbar* of ebony andsandalwood.

No Christian footstep has yet profaned Kairouiyin, but fairly definiteinformation as to its plan has been gleaned by students of Moroccan art.the number of its "countless" columns has been counted, and it is knownthat, to the right of the *mirhab*, carved cedar doors open into amortuary chapel called "the mosque of the dead"—and also that in thischapel, on Fridays, old books and precious manuscripts are sold byauction.

This odd association of uses recalls the fact that Kairouiyin is notonly a church but a library, the University of Fez as well as itscathedral. The beautiful Medersas with which the Merinids adorned thecity are simply the lodging-houses of the students; the classes are allheld in the courts and galleries adjoining the mosque.

El Kairouiyin was originally an oratory built in the ninth century byFatmah, whose father had migrated from Kairouan to Fez. Later it wasenlarged, and its cupola was surmounted by the talismans which protectsacred edifices against rats, scorpions and serpents; but in spite ofthese precautions all animal life was not successfully exorcised fromit. In the twelfth century, when the great gate Ech Chemmâïn wasbuilding, a well was discovered under its foundations. The mouth of thewell was obstructed by an immense tortoise; but when the workmenattempted to take the tortoise out she said: "Burn me rather than takeme away from here." They respected her wishes and built her into thefoundations; and since then women who suffer from the back-ache haveonly to come and sit on the bench above the well to be cured.

The actual mosque, or "praying-hall," is said to be formed of arectangle or double cube of 90 metres by 45, and this vast space isequally divided by rows of horseshoe arches resting on whitewashed pierson which the lower part is swathed in finely patterned matting fromSalé. Fifteen monumental doorways lead into the mosque. Their doors areof cedar, heavily barred and ornamented with wrought iron, and one ofthem bears the name of the artisan, and the date 531 of the Hegira (thefirst half of the twelfth century). The mosque also contains the twohalls of audience of the Cadi, of which one has a graceful exteriorfaçade with coupled lights under horseshoe arches; the library, whose20,000 volumes are reported to have dwindled to about a thousand; thechapel where the Masters of the Koran recite the sacred text infulfilment of pious bequests; the "museum" in the upper part of theminaret, wherein a remarkable collection of ancient astronomicalinstruments is said to be preserved; and the *mestonda*, or raised hallabove the court, where women come to pray.

But the crown of El Kairouiyin is the Merinid court of ablutions. Thisinaccessible wonder lies close under the Medersa Attarine, one of theoldest and most beautiful collegiate buildings of Fez; and through thekindness of the Director of Fine Arts, who was with us, we were takenup to the roof of the Medersa and allowed to look down into theenclosure.

It is so closely guarded from below that from our secret of vantage weseemed to be looking down into the heart of forbidden things. Spaciousand serene the great tiled cloister lay beneath us, water spilling overfrom a central basin of marble with a cool sound to which lesserfountains made answer from under the pyramidal green roofs of the twinpavilions. It was near the prayer-hour, and worshippers were flockingin, laying off their shoes and burnouses, washing their faces at thefountains and their feet in the central tank, or stretching themselvesout in the shadow of the enclosing arcade.

This, then, was the famous court "so cool in the great heats that seatedby thy beautiful jet of water I feel the perfection of bliss"—as thelearned doctor Abou Abd Allah el Maghili sang of it; the court in whichthe students gather from the adjoining halls after having committed tomemory the principals of grammar in prose and verse, the "science ofthe reading of the Koran," the invention, exposition and ornaments ofstyle, law, medicine, theology, metaphysics and astronomy, as well asthe talismanic numbers, and the art of ascertaining by calculation theinfluences of the angels, the spirits and the heavenly bodies, "thenames of the victor and the vanquished, and of the desired object andthe person who desires it."

Such is the twentieth-century curriculum of the University of Fez.Repetition is the rule of Arab education as it is of Arab ornament. Theteaching of the University is based entirely on the mediæval principleof mnemonics; and as there are no examinations, no degrees, no limits tothe duration of any given course, nor is any disgrace attached toslowness in learning, it is not surprising that many students, coming asyouths, linger by the fountain of Kairouiyin till their hair is gray.One well-known *oulama* has lately finished his studies aftertwenty-seven years at the University, and is justly proud of the lengthof his stay. The life of the scholar is easy, the way of knowledge islong, the contrast exquisite between the foul lanes and noisy bazaarsoutside and this cool heaven of learning. No wonder the students ofKairouiyin say with the tortoise: "Burn me rather than take me away."

IV

EL ANDALOUS AND THE POTTERS' FIELD

Outside the sacred precincts of Moulay Idriss and Kairouiyin, on theother side of the Oued Fez, lies El Andalous, the mosque which theAndalusian Moors built when they settled in Fez in the ninth century.

It stands apart from the bazaars, on higher ground, and though it is not*horm* we found it less easy to see than the more famous mosques, sincethe Christian loiterer in its doorways is more quickly noticed. The Faziare not yet used to seeing unbelievers near their sacred places. It isonly in the tumult and confusion of the *souks* that one can linger onthe edge of the inner mysteries without becoming aware of attractingsullen looks; and my only impression of El Andalous is of a magnificentAlmohad door and the rich blur of an interior in which there was no timeto single out the details.

Turning from its forbidden and forbidding threshold we rode on througha poor quarter which leads to the great gate of Bab F'touh. Beyond thegate rises a dusty rocky slope extending to the outer walls—one ofthose grim intramural deserts that girdle Fez with desolation. This oneis strewn with gravestones, not enclosed, but, as in most Moroccancemeteries, simply cropping up like nettles between the rocks and out ofthe flaming dust. Here and there among the slabs rises a well-curb or acrumbling *koubba*. A solitary palm shoots up beside one of the shrines.And between the crowded graves the caravan trail crosses from the outerto the inner gate, and perpetual lines of camels and donkeys trample thedead a little deeper into the dusty earth.

This Bab F'touh cemetery is also a kind of fondak. Poor caravans campthere under the walls in a mire of offal and chicken-feathers andstripped date-branches prowled through by wolfish dogs and buzzed overby fat blue flies. Camel-drivers squat beside iron kettles over heaps ofembers, sorcerers from the Sahara offer their amulets to negro women,peddlers with portable wooden booths sell greasy cakes that look as ifthey had been made out of the garbage of the caravans, and in and outamong the unknown dead and sleeping saints circulates the squalidindifferent life of the living poor.

A walled lane leads down from Bab F'touh to a lower slope, where theFazi potters have their baking-kilns. Under a series of grassy terracesovergrown with olives we saw the archaic ovens and dripping wheels whichproduce the earthenware sold in the *souks*. It is a primitive andhomely ware, still fine in shape, though dull in color and monotonous inpattern; and stacked on the red earth under the olives, the rows of jarsand cups, in their unglazed and unpainted state, showed their classicaldescent more plainly than after they have been decorated.

This green quiet hollow, where turbaned figures were moving attentivelyamong the primitive ovens, so near to the region of flies and offal wehad just left, woke an old phrase in our memories, and as our mulesstumbled back over the graves of Bab F'touh we understood the grimmeaning of the words: "They carried him out and buried him in thePotters' Field."

V

MEDERSAS, BAZAARS AND AN OASIS

Fez, for two centuries and more, was in a double sense the capital ofMorocco: the centre of its trade as well as of its culture.

Culture, in fact, came to northwest Africa chiefly through the Merinidprinces. The Almohads had erected great monuments from Rabat toMarrakech, and had fortified Fez; but their "mighty wasteful empire"fell apart like those that had preceded it. Stability had to come fromthe west; it was not till the Arabs had learned it through the Moorsthat Morocco produced a dynasty strong and enlightened enough to carryout the dream of its founders.

Whichever way the discussion sways as to the priority of eastern orwestern influences on Moroccan art—whether it came to her from Syria,and was thence passed on to Spain, or was first formed in Spain, andafterward modified by the Moroccan imagination—there can at least be nodoubt that Fazi art and culture, in their prime, are partly thereflection of European civilization.

Fugitives from Spain came to the new city when Moulay Idriss foundedit. One part of the town was given to them, and the river divided theElbali of the Almohads into the two quarters of Kairouiyin and Andalous,which still retain their old names. But the full intellectual andartistic flowering of Fez was delayed till the thirteenth and fourteenthcenturies. It seems as though the seeds of the new springtime of art,blown across the sea from reawakening Europe, had at last given theweltering tribes of the desert the force to create their own type ofbeauty.

Nine Medersas sprang up in Fez, six of them built by the princes whowere also creating the exquisite collegiate buildings of Salé, Rabat andold Meknez, and the enchanting mosque and minaret of Chella. The powerof these rulers also was in perpetual flux; they were always at war withthe Sultans of Tlemeen, the Christians of Spain, the princes of northernAlgeria and Tunis. But during the fourteenth century they established arule wide and firm enough to permit of the great outburst of art andlearning which produced the Medersas of Fez.

Until a year or two ago these collegiate buildings were as inaccessibleas the mosques; but now that the French government has undertaken theirrestoration strangers may visit them under the guidance of the Fine ArtsDepartment.

All are built on the same plan, the plan of Salé and Rabat, which (as M.Tranchant de Lunel has pointed out) became, with slightmodifications, that of the rich private houses of Morocco. Butinteresting as they are in plan and the application of ornament, theirmain beauty lies in their details: in the union of chiselled plasterwith the delicate mosaic work of niches and revêtements; the web-likearabesques of the upper walls and the bold, almost Gothic sculpture ofthe cedar architraves and corbels supporting them. And when all thesedetails are enumerated, and also the fretted panels of cedar, the bronzedoors with their great shield-like bosses, and the honeycombings andrufflings of the gilded ceilings, there still remains the general tingeof dry disintegration, as though all were perishing of a desertfever—that, and the final wonder of seeing before one, in such asetting, the continuance of the very life that went on there when thetiles were set and the gold was new on the ceilings.

For these tottering Medersas, already in the hands of the restorers, arestill inhabited. As long as the stairway holds and the balcony has notrotted from its corbels, the students of the University see no reasonfor abandoning their lodgings above the cool fountain and the house ofprayer. The strange men giving incomprehensible orders for unnecessaryrepairs need not disturb their meditations; and when the hammering growstoo loud the *oulamas* have only to pass through the silk market or the*souk* of the embroiderers to the mosque of Kairouiyin, and go onweaving the pattern of their dreams by the fountain of perfect bliss.

*   *   *   *   *

One reads of the bazaars of Fez that they have been for centuries thecentral market of the country. Here are to be found not only the silksand pottery, the Jewish goldsmiths' work, the arms and embroideredsaddlery which the city itself produces, but "morocco" from Marrakech,rugs, tent-hangings and matting from Rabat and Salé, grain baskets fromMoulay Idriss, daggers from the Souss, and whatever European wares thenative markets consume. One looks, on the plan of Fez, at the spacecovered by the bazaars; one breasts the swarms that pour through themfrom dawn to dusk—and one remains perplexed, disappointed. They areless "Oriental" than one had expected, if "Oriental" means color andgaiety.

Sometimes, on occasion, it does mean that: as, for instance, when aprocession passes bearing the gifts for a Jewish wedding. The gray crowdmakes way for a group of musicians in brilliant caftans, and followingthem comes a long file of women with uncovered faces and bejewellednecks, balancing on their heads the dishes the guests have sent to thefeast—*kouskous*, sweet creams and syrups, "gazelles' horns" of sugarand almonds—in delicately woven baskets, each covered with severalsquares of bright gauze edged with gold. Then one remembers themarketing of the Lady of "The Three Calendars," and Fez again becomesthe Bagdad of Al Raschid.

But when no exceptional events, processions, ceremonies and the likebrighten the underworld of the *souks*, their look is uniformlymelancholy. The gay bazaars, the gaily-painted houses, the flowers andflute-playing of North Africa, are found in her Mediterranean ports, incontact with European influences. The farther west she extends, the moreshe becomes self-contained, sombre, uninfluenced, a gloomy fanatic withher back to the walls of the Atlantic and the Atlas. Color and laughterlie mostly along the trade-routes, where the peoples of the world comeand go in curiosity and rivalry. This ashen crowd swarming gloomilythrough the dark tunnels represents the real Moghreb that is close tothe wild tribes of the "hinterland" and the grim feudal fortresses ofthe Atlas. How close, one has only to go out to Sefrou on a market-dayto see.

Sefrou is a military outpost in an oasis under the Atlas, about fortymiles south of Fez. To most people the word "oasis" evokes palms andsand; but though Morocco possesses many oases it has no pure sand andfew palms. I remember it as a considerable event when I discovered onefrom my lofty window at Bou-Jeloud.

The *bled* is made of very different stuff from the sand-ocean of theSahara. The light plays few tricks with it. Its monotony is wearisomerather than impressive, and the fact that it is seldom without some formof dwarfish vegetation makes the transition less startling when thealluvial green is finally reached. One had always half expected it, andit does not spring at a djinn's wave out of sterile gold.

But the fact brings its own compensations. Moroccan oases differ onefrom another far more than those of South Algeria and Tunisia. Some haveno palms, others but a few, others are real palm-oases, though even inthe south (at least on the hither side of the great Atlas) none spreadsout a dense uniform roofing of metal-blue fronds like the date-oases ofBiskra or Tozeur. As for Sefrou, which Foucauld called the mostbeautiful oasis of Morocco, it is simply an extremely fertile valleywith vineyards and orchards stretching up to a fine background ofmountains. But the fact that it lies just below the Atlas makes it animportant market-place and centre of caravans.

Though so near Fez it is still almost on the disputed border between theloyal and the "unsubmissive" tribes, those that are *Blad-Makhzen* (ofthe Sultan's government) and those that are against it. Until recently,therefore, it has been inaccessible to visitors, and even now a stronglyfortified French post dominates the height above the town. Looking downfrom the fort, one distinguishes, through masses of many-tinted green, asuburb of Arab houses in gardens, and below, on the river, Sefrouitself, a stout little walled town with angle-towers defiantly thrustforth toward the Atlas. It is just outside these walls that the marketis held.

It was swarming with hill-people the day we were there, and strange wasthe contrast between the crowd inside the circle of picketed horses andthe white-robed cockneys from Rabat who fill the market-place of Salé.Here at last we were in touch with un-Arab Morocco, with Berbers of the*bled* and the hills, whose women know no veils and no seclusion, andwho, under a thin surface of Mahometanism, preserve their old stone andanimal worship, and all the gross fetichistic beliefs from which Mahometdreamed of freeing Africa.

The men were lean and weather-bitten, some with negroid lips, otherswith beaked noses and gaunt cheek-bones, all muscular andfierce-looking. Some were wrapped in the black cloaks worn by the BlueMen of the Sahara, with a great orange sun embroidered on the back;some tunicked like the Egyptian fellah, under a rough striped outergarment trimmed with bright tufts and tassels of wool. The men of theRif had a braided lock on the shoulder, those of the Atlas a ringletover each ear, and brown woollen scarfs wound round their temples,leaving the shaven crown bare.

The women, squatting among their kids and poultry and cheeses, glancedat us with brilliant hennaed eyes and smiles that lifted their shortupper lips maliciously. Their thin faces were painted in stripes andpatterns of indigo. Silver necklets covered their throats, long earringsdangled under the wool-embroidered kerchiefs bound about their templeswith a twist of camel's hair, and below the cotton shifts fastened ontheir shoulders with silver clasps their legs were bare to the knee, orcovered with leather leggings to protect them from the thorny *bled*.

They seemed abler bargainers than the men, and the play of expression ontheir dramatic and intensely feminine faces as they wheedled the priceof a calf out of a fierce hillsman, or haggled over a heap of dates thata Jew with greasy ringlets was trying to secure for his secretdistillery, showed that they knew their superiority and enjoyed it.

Jews abounded in the market-place and also in the town. Sefrou containsa large Israelite colony, and after we had wandered through the steepstreets, over gushing waterfalls spanned by "ass-backed" Spanishbridges, and through a thatched *souk* smelling strong of camels and thedesert, the French commissioner (the only European in Sefrou) suggestedthat it might interest us to visit the *Mellah*.

It was our first sight of a typical Jewish quarter in Africa. The*Mellah* of Fez was almost entirely destroyed during the massacres of1912 (which incidentally included a *pogrom*), and its distinctivecharacter, happily for the inhabitants, has disappeared in therebuilding. North African Jews are still compelled to live in ghettos,into which they are locked at night, as in France and Germany in theMiddle Ages; and until lately the men have been compelled to go unarmed,to wear black gabardines and black slippers, to take off their shoeswhen they passed near a mosque or a saint's tomb, and in various otherways to manifest their subjection to the ruling race. Nowhere else dothey live in conditions of such demoralizing promiscuity as in some ofthe cities of Morocco. They have so long been subject to unrestrictedextortion on the part of the Moslems that even the wealthy Jews (who arenumerous) have sunk to the habits and appearance of the poorest; andSefrou, which has come so recently under French control, offers a goodspecimen of a *Mellah* before foreign sanitation has lighted up its darkplaces.

Dark indeed they were. After wandering through narrow and malodorouslanes, and slipping about in the offal of the *souks*, we were suddenlyled under an arch over which should have been written "All lightabandon—" and which made all we had seen before seem clean and brightand airy.

The beneficent African sun dries up and purifies the immemorial filthof Africa; where that sun enters there is none of the foulness of damp.But into the *Mellah* of Sefrou it never comes, for the streets form asort of subterranean rabbit-warren under the upper stories of a solidagglomeration of tall houses—a buried city lit even at midday byoil-lamps hanging in the goldsmiths' shops and under the archways of theblack and reeking staircases.

It was a Jewish feast-day. The Hebrew stalls in the *souks* were closed, and the whole population of the *Mellah* thronged its tunnels in holiday dress. Hurrying past us were young women with plump white faces and lovely eyes, turbaned in brilliant gauzes, with draperies of dirty curtain muslin over tawdry brocaded caftans. Their paler children swarmed about them, little long-earringed girls like wax dolls dressed in scraps of old finery, little boys in tattered caftans with long-lashed eyes and wily smiles; and, waddling in the rear, their unwieldy grandmothers, huge lumps of tallowy flesh who were probably still in the thirties.

With them were the men of the family, in black gabardines and skull-caps: sallow striplings, incalculably aged ancestors, round-bellied husbands and fathers bumping along like black balloons; all hastening to the low doorways dressed with lamps and paper garlands behind which the feast was spread.

One is told that in cities like Fez and Marrakech the Hebrew quarter conceals flowery patios and gilded rooms with the heavy European furniture that rich Jews delight in. Perhaps even in the *Mellah* of Sefrou, among the ragged figures shuffling past us, there were some few with bags of gold in their walls and rich stuffs hid away in painted coffers; but for patios and flowers and daylight there seemed no room in the dark *bolgia* they inhabit. No wonder the babies of the Moroccan ghettos are nursed on date-brandy, and their elders doze away to death under its consoling spell.

VI
THE LAST GLIMPSE

It is well to bid good-by to Fez at night—a moonlight night for choice.

Then, after dining at the Arab inn of Fez Eldjid—where it might be inconvenient to lodge, but where it is extremely pleasant to eat *kouskous* under a grape-trellis in a tiled and fountained patio—this pleasure over, one may set out on foot and stray down the lanes toward Fez Elbali.

Not long ago the gates between the different quarters of the city used to be locked every night at nine o'clock, and the merchant who went out to dine in another part of the town had to lodge with his host. Now this custom has been given up, and one may roam about untroubled through the old quarters, grown as silent as the grave after the intense life of the bazaars has ceased at nightfall.

Nobody is in the streets: wandering from ghostly passage to passage, onehears no step but that of the watchman with staff and lantern. Presentlythere appears, far off, a light like a low-flying firefly; as it comesnearer, it is seen to proceed from the *Mellah* lamp of open-work brassthat a servant carries ahead of two merchants on their way home fromElbali. The merchants are grave men: they move softly and slowly ontheir fat slippered feet, pausing from time to time in confidentialtalk. At last they stop before a house wall with a low blue door barredby heavy hasps of iron. The servant lifts the lamp and knocks. There isa long delay; then, with infinite caution, the door is opened a fewinches, and another lifted light shines faintly on lustrous tiled walls,and on the face of a woman slave who quickly veils herself. Evidentlythe master is a man of standing, and the house well guarded. The twomerchants touch each other on the right shoulder, one of them passes in,and his friend goes on through the moonlight, his servant's lanterndancing ahead.

But here we are in an open space looking down one of the descents to ElAttarine. A misty radiance washes the tall houses, the garden-walls, thearchways; even the moonlight does not whiten Fez, but only turns itsgray to tarnished silver. Overhead in a tower window a single lighttwinkles: women's voices rise and fall on the roofs. In a rich man'sdoorway slaves are sleeping, huddled on the tiles. A cock crows fromsomebody's dunghill; a skeleton dog prowls by for garbage.

Everywhere is the loud rush or the low crooning of water, and over everywall comes the scent of jasmine and rose. Far off, from the redpurgatory between the walls, sounds the savage thrum-thrum of a negroorgy; here all is peace and perfume. A minaret springs up between theroof like a palm, and from its balcony the little white figure bendsover and drops a blessing on all the loveliness and all the squalor.

IV
MARRAKECH

I

THE WAY THERE

There are countless Arab tales of evil Djinns who take the form ofsandstorms and hot winds to overwhelm exhausted travellers.

In spite of the new French road between Rabat and Marrakech the memoryof such tales rises up insistently from every mile of the level redearth and the desolate stony stretches of the *bled*. As long as theroad runs in sight of the Atlantic breakers they give the scenefreshness and life; but when it bends inland and stretches away acrossthe wilderness the sense of the immensity and immobility of Africadescends on one with an intolerable oppression.

The road traverses no villages, and not even a ring of nomad tents isvisible in the distance on the wide stretches of arable land. Atinfrequent intervals our motor passed a train of laden mules, or a groupof peasants about a well, and sometimes, far off, a fortified farmprofiled its thick-set angle-towers against the sky, or a white *koubba*floated like a mirage above the brush; but these rare signs of lifeintensified the solitude of the long miles between.

At midday we were refreshed by the sight of the little oasis around themilitary-post of Settat. We lunched there with the commanding officer,in a cool Arab house about a flowery patio; but that brief intervalover, the fiery plain began again. After Settat the road runs on formiles across the waste to the gorge of the Oued Ouem; and beyond theriver it climbs to another plain so desperate in its calcined ariditythat the prickly scrub of the wilderness we had left seemed like thevegetation of an oasis. For fifty kilometres the earth under our wheelswas made up of a kind of glistening red slag covered with pebbles andstones. Not the scantest and toughest of rock-growths thrust a leafthrough its brassy surface; not a well-head or a darker depression ofthe rock gave sign of a trickle of water. Everything around us glitteredwith the same unmerciful dryness.

A long way ahead loomed the line of the Djebilets, the Djinn-haunted mountains guarding Marrakech on the north. When at last we reached them the wicked glister of their purple flanks seemed like a volcanic upheaval of the plain. For some time we had watched the clouds gathering over them, and as we got to the top of the defile rain was falling from a fringe of thunder to the south. Then the vapours lifted, and we saw below us another red plain with an island of palms in its centre. Mysteriously, from the heart of the palms, a tower shot up, as if alone in the wilderness; behind it stood the sun-streaked cliffs of the Atlas, with snow summits appearing and vanishing through the storm.

As we drove downward the rock gradually began to turn to red earth fissured by yellow streams, and stray knots of palms sprang up, lean and dishevelled, about well-heads where people were watering camels and donkeys. To the east, dominating the oasis, the twin peaked hills of the Ghilis, fortified to the crest, mounted guard over invisible Marrakech; but still, above the palms, we saw only that lonely and triumphant tower.

Presently we crossed the Oued Tensif on an old bridge built by Moroccan engineers. Beyond the river were more palms, then olive-orchards, then the vague sketch of the new European settlement, with a few shops and cafés on avenues ending suddenly in clay pits, and at last Marrakech itself appeared to us, in the form of a red wall across a red wilderness.

We passed through a gate and were confronted by other ramparts. Then we entered an outskirt of dusty red lanes bordered by clay hovels with draped figures slinking by like ghosts. After that more walls, more gates, more endlessly winding lanes, more gates again, more turns, a dusty open space with donkeys and camels and negroes; a final wall with a great door under a lofty arch—and suddenly we were in the palace of the Bahia, among flowers and shadows and falling water.

II

THE BAHIA

Whoever would understand Marrakech must begin by mounting at sunset to the roof of the Bahia.

Outspread below lies the oasis-city of the south, flat and vast as the great nomad camp it really is, its low roofs extending on all sides to a belt of blue palms ringed with desert. Only two or three minarets and a few noblemen's houses among gardens break the general flatness; but they are hardly noticeable, so irresistibly is the eye drawn toward two dominant objects—the white wall of the Atlas and the red tower of the Koutoubya.

Foursquare, untapering, the great tower lifts its flanks of ruddy stone. Its large spaces of unornamented wall, its triple tier of clustered openings, lightening as they rise from the severe rectangular lights of the first stage to the graceful arcade below the parapet, have the stern harmony of the noblest architecture. The Koutoubya would be magnificent anywhere; in this flat desert it is grand enough to face the Atlas.

The Almohad conquerors who built the Koutoubya and embellished Marrakech dreamed a dream of beauty that extended from the Guadalquivir to the Sahara; and at its two extremes they placed their watch-towers. The Giralda watched over civilized enemies in a land of ancient Roman culture; the Koutoubya stood at the edge of the world, facing the hordes of the desert.

The Almoravid princes who founded Marrakech came from the black desert of Senegal; themselves were leaders of wild hordes. In the history of North Africa the same cycle has perpetually repeated itself. Generation after generation of chiefs have flowed in from the desert or the mountains, overthrown their predecessors, massacred, plundered, grown rich, built sudden palaces, encouraged their great servants to do the same; then fallen on them, and taken their wealth and their palaces. Usually some religious fury, some ascetic wrath against the self-indulgence of the cities, has been the motive of these attacks; but invariably the same results followed, as they followed when the Germanic barbarians descended on Italy. The conquerors, infected with luxury and mad with power, built vaster palaces, planned grander cities; but Sultans and Viziers camped in their golden houses as if on the march, and the mud huts of the tribesmen within their walls were but one degree removed from the mud-walled tents of the *bled*.

This was more especially the case with Marrakech, a city of Berbers and blacks, and the last outpost against the fierce black world beyond the Atlas from which its founders came. When one looks at its site, and considers its history, one can only marvel at the height of civilization it attained.

The Bahia itself, now the palace of the Resident General, though builtless than a hundred years ago, is typical of the architecturalmegalomania of the great southern chiefs. It was built by Ba-Ahmed, theall-powerful black Vizier of the Sultan Moulay-el-Hassan. Ba-Ahmedwas evidently an artist and an archæologist. His ambition was tore-create a Palace of Beauty such as the Moors had built in the prime ofArab art, and he brought to Marrakech skilled artificers of Fez, thelast surviving masters of the mystery of chiselled plaster and ceramicmosaics and honeycombing of gilded cedar. They came, they built theBahia, and it remains the loveliest and most fantastic of Moroccanpalaces.

Court within court, garden beyond garden, reception halls, privateapartments, slaves' quarters, sunny prophets' chambers on the roofs andbaths in vaulted crypts, the labyrinth of passages and rooms stretchesaway over several acres of ground. A long court enclosed in pale-greentrellis-work, where pigeons plume themselves about a great tank and thedripping tiles glitter with refracted sunlight, leads to the fresh gloomof a cypress garden, or under jasmine tunnels bordered with runningwater; and these again open on arcaded apartments faced with tiles andstucco-work, where, in a languid twilight, the hours drift by to theceaseless music of the fountains.

The beauty of Moroccan palaces is made up of details of ornament andrefinements of sensuous delight too numerous to record; but to get anidea of their general character it is worth while to cross the Court ofCypresses at the Bahia and follow a series of low-studded passages thatturn on themselves till they reach the centre of the labyrinth. Here,passing by a low padlocked door leading to a crypt, and known as the"Door of the Vizier's Treasure-House," one comes on a painted portalthat opens into a still more secret sanctuary: The apartment of theGrand Vizier's Favourite.

This lovely prison, from which all sight and sound of the outer worldare excluded, is built about an atrium paved with disks of turquoise andblack and white. Water trickles from a central *vasca* of alabaster intoa hexagonal mosaic channel in the pavement. The walls, which are atleast twenty-five feet high, are roofed with painted beams resting onpanels of traceried stucco in which is set a clerestory of jewelledglass. On each side of the atrium are long recessed rooms closed byvermilion doors painted with gold arabesques and vases of springflowers; and into these shadowy inner rooms, spread with rugs and divansand soft pillows, no light comes except when their doors are openedinto the atrium. In this fabulous place it was my good luck to be lodgedwhile I was at Marrakech.

In a climate where, after the winter snow has melted from the Atlas,every breath of air for long months is a flame of fire, these enclosedrooms in the middle of the palaces are the only places of refuge fromthe heat. Even in October the temperature of the favourite's apartmentwas deliciously reviving after a morning in the bazaars or the dustystreets, and I never came back to its wet tiles and perpetual twilightwithout the sense of plunging into a deep sea-pool.

From far off, through circuitous corridors, came the scent ofcitron-blossom and jasmine, with sometimes a bird's song before dawn,sometimes a flute's wail at sunset, and always the call of the muezzinin the night; but no sunlight reached the apartment except in remoterays through the clerestory, and no air except through one or two brokenpanes.

Sometimes, lying on my divan, and looking out through the vermiliondoors, I used to surprise a pair of swallows dropping down from theirnest in the cedar-beams to preen themselves on the fountain's edge or inthe channels of the pavement; for the roof was full of birds who cameand went through the broken panes of the clerestory. Usually they weremy only visitors; but one morning just at daylight I was waked by a softtramp of bare feet, and saw, silhouetted against the cream-colouredwalls, a procession of eight tall negroes in linen tunics, who filednoiselessly across the atrium like a moving frieze of bronze. In thatfantastic setting, and the hush of that twilight hour, the vision was solike the picture of a "Seraglio Tragedy," some fragment of a Delacroixor Decamps floating up into the drowsy brain, that I almost fancied Ihad seen the ghosts of Ba-Ahmed's executioners revisiting with daggerand bowstring the scene of an unavenged crime.

A cock crew, and they vanished ... and when I made the mistake ofasking what they had been doing in my room at that hour I was told (asthough it were the most natural thing in the world) that they were themunicipal lamp-lighters of Marrakech, whose duty it is to refill everymorning the two hundred acetylene lamps lighting the palace of theResident General. Such unforeseen aspects, in this mysterious city, dothe most ordinary domestic functions wear.

III

THE BAZAARS

Passing out of the enchanted circle of the Bahia it is startling to plunge into the native life about its gates.

Marrakech is the great market of the south; and the south means not only the Atlas with its feudal chiefs and their wild clansmen, but all that lies beyond of heat and savagery: the Sahara of the veiled Touaregs, Dakka, Timbuctoo, Senegal and the Soudan. Here come the camel caravans from Demnat and Tameslout, from the Moulouya and the Souss, and those from the Atlantic ports and the confines of Algeria. The population of this old city of the southern march has always been even more mixed than that of the northerly Moroccan towns. It is made up of the descendants of all the peoples conquered by a long line of Sultans who brought their trains of captives across the sea from Moorish Spain and across the Sahara from Timbuctoo. Even in the highly cultivated region on the lower slopes of the Atlas there are groups of varied ethnic origin, the descendants of tribes transplanted by long-gone rulers and still preserving many of their original characteristics.

In the bazaars all these peoples meet and mingle: cattle-dealers, olive-growers, peasants from the Atlas, the Souss and the Draa, Blue Men of the Sahara, blacks from Senegal and the Soudan, coming in to trade with the wool-merchants, tanners, leather-merchants, silk-weavers, armourers, and makers of agricultural implements.

Dark, fierce and fanatical are these narrow *souks* of Marrakech. They are mere mud lanes roofed with rushes, as in South Tunisia and Timbuctoo, and the crowds swarming in them are so dense that it is hardly possible, at certain hours, to approach the tiny raised kennels where the merchants sit like idols among their wares. One feels at once that something more than the thought of bargaining—dear as this is to the African heart—animates these incessantly moving throngs. The Souks of Marrakech seem, more than any others, the central organ of a native life that extends far beyond the city walls into secret clefts of the mountains and far-off oases where plots are hatched and holy wars fomented—farther still, to yellow deserts whence negroes are secretly brought across the Atlas to that inmost recess of the bazaar where the ancient traffic in flesh and blood still surreptitiously goes on.

All these many threads of the native life, woven of greed and lust, offetichism and fear and blind hate of the stranger, form, in the *souks*, a thick network in which at times one's feet seem literally to stumble.Fanatics in sheepskins glowering from the guarded thresholds of themosques, fierce tribesmen with inlaid arms in their belts and thefighters' tufts of wiry hair escaping from camel's-hair turbans, madnegroes standing stark naked in niches of the walls and pouring downSoudanese incantations upon the fascinated crowd, consumptive Jews withpathos and cunning in their large eyes and smiling lips, lustyslave-girls with earthen oil-jars resting against swaying hips,almond-eyed boys leading fat merchants by the hand, and bare-leggedBerber women, tattooed and insolently gay, trading their stripedblankets, or bags of dried roses and irises, for sugar, tea orManchester cottons—from all these hundreds of unknown and unknowablepeople, bound together by secret affinities, or intriguing against eachother with secret hate, there emanates an atmosphere of mystery andmenace more stifling than the smell of camels and spices and blackbodies and smoking fry which hangs like a fog under the close roofing ofthe *souks*.

And suddenly one leaves the crowd and the turbid air for one of thosequiet corners that are like the back-waters of the bazaars: a smallsquare where a vine stretches across a shop-front and hangs ripeclusters of grapes through the reeds. In the patterning of grape-shadowsa very old donkey, tethered to a stone-post, dozes under a pack-saddlethat is never taken off; and near by, in a matted niche, sits a very oldman in white. This is the chief of the Guild of "morocco" workers ofMarrakech, the most accomplished craftsman in Morocco in the preparingand using of the skins to which the city gives its name. Of these sleekmoroccos, cream-white or dyed with cochineal or pomegranate skins, aremade the rich bags of the Chleuh dancing-boys, the embroidered slippersfor the harem, the belts and harnesses that figure so largely inMoroccan trade—and of the finest, in old days, were made thepomegranate-red morocco bindings of European bibliophiles.

From this peaceful corner one passes into the barbaric splendor of asouk hung with innumerable plumy bunches of floss silk—skeins ofcitron yellow, crimson, grasshopper green and pure purple. This is thesilk-spinners' quarter, and next to it comes that of the dyers, withgreat seething vats into which the raw silk is plunged, and ropeso. . .head where the rainbow masses are hung out to dry.

Another turn leads into the street of the metalworkers and armourers,where the sunlight through the thatch flames on round flanks of beatencopper or picks out the silver bosses of ornate powder-flasks andpistols; and near by is the *souk* of the plough-shares, crowded withpeasants in rough Chleuh cloaks who are waiting to have their archaicploughs repaired, and that of the smiths, in an outer lane of mud hutswhere negroes squat in the dust and sinewy naked figures in tatteredloincloths bend over blazing coals. And here ends the maze of thebazaars.

IV

THE AGDAL

One of the Almohad Sultans who, during their hundred years of empire,scattered such great monuments from Seville to the Atlas, felt the needof coolness about his southern capital, and laid out the olive-yards ofthe Agdal.

To the south of Marrakech the Agdal extends for many acres between theouter walls of the city and the edge of the palm-oasis—a continuousbelt of silver foliage traversed by deep red lanes, and enclosing awide-spreading summer palace and two immense reservoirs walled withmasonry; and the vision of these serene sheets of water, in which theolives and palms are motionlessly reflected, is one of the most poeticimpressions in that city of inveterate poetry.

On the edge of one of the reservoirs a sentimental Sultan built in thelast century a little pleasure-house called the Menara. It is composedof a few rooms with a two-storied loggia looking across the water to thepalm-groves, and surrounded by a garden of cypresses and orange-trees.The Menara, long since abandoned, is usually uninhabited; but on the daywhen we drove through the Agdal we noticed, at the gate, a group ofwell-dressed servants holding mules with embroidered saddle-clothes.

The French officer who was with us asked the porter what was going on,and he replied that the Chief of the Guild of Wool-Merchants had hiredthe pavilion for a week and invited a few friends to visit him. Theywere now, the porter added, taking tea in the loggia above the lake; andthe host,

being informed of our presence, begged that we should do him and his friends
the honour of visiting the pavilion.

In reply to this amiable invitation we crossed an empty saloon surrounded
with divans and passed out onto the loggia where the wool-merchant and his
guests were seated. They were evidently persons of consequence: large bulky
men wrapped in fresh muslins and reclining side by side on muslin-covered
divans and cushions. Black slaves had placed before them brass trays with pots
of mint-tea, glasses in filigree stands, and dishes of gazelles' horns and
sugar-plums; and they sat serenely absorbing these refreshments and gazing
with large calm eyes upon the motionless water and the reflected trees.

So, we were told, they would probably spend the greater part of
their holiday. The merchant's cooks had taken possession of the kitchens,
and toward sunset a sumptuous repast of many courses would be carried
into the saloon on covered trays, and the guests would squat about it on rugs of
Rabat, tearing with their fingers the tender chicken wings and
small artichokes cooked in oil, plunging their fat white hands to the wrist into
huge mounds of saffron and rice, and washing off the traces of each course in
the brass basin of perfumed water carried about by a young black slave-girl
with hoop-earrings and a green-and-gold scarf about her hips.

Then the singing-girls would come out from Marrakech, squat
round-faced young women heavily hennaed and bejewelled, accompanied by
gaunt musicians in bright caftans; and for hours they would sing sentimental or
obscene ballads to the persistent maddening twang of violin and flute and
drum. Meanwhile fiery brandy or sweet champagne would probably be passed
around between the steaming glasses of mint-tea which the slaves perpetually
refilled; or perhaps the sultry air, the heavy meal, the scent of the garden and
the vertiginous repetition of the music would suffice to plunge these sedentary
worthies into the delicious coma in which every festive evening in Morocco
ends.

The next day would be spent in the same manner, except that probably
the Chleuh boys with sidelong eyes and clean caftans would come instead
of the singing-girls, and weave the arabesque of their dance in place of the
runic pattern of the singing. But the result would always be the same: a
prolonged state of obese ecstasy culminating in the collapse of huge heaps of

snoring muslin on the divans against the wall. Finally atthe week's end the wool-merchant and his friends would all ride backwith dignity to the bazaar.

V
ON THE ROOFS

"Should you like to see the Chleuh boys dance?" some one asked.

"There they are," another of our companions added, pointing to a densering of spectators on one side of the immense dusty square at theentrance of the *souks*—the "Square of the Dead" as it is called, inmemory of the executions that used to take place under one of its grimred gates.

It is the square of the living now, the centre of all the life,amusement and gossip of Marrakech, and the spectators are so thicklypacked about the story-tellers, snake-charmers and dancers who frequentit that one can guess what is going on within each circle only by thewailing monologue or the persistent drum-beat that proceeds from it.

Ah, yes—we should indeed like to see the Chleuh boys dance; we who,since we had been in Morocco, had seen no dancing, heard no singing,caught no single glimpse of merry-making! But how were we to get withinsight of them?

On one side of the "Square of the Dead" stands a large house, ofEuropean build, but modelled on Oriental lines: the office of the Frenchmunicipal administration. The French Government no longer allows itsoffices to be built within the walls of Moroccan towns, and this housegoes back to the epic days of the Caïd Sir Harry Maclean, to whom it waspresented by the fantastic Abd-el-Aziz when the Caïd was his favouritecompanion as well as his military adviser.

At the suggestion of the municipal officials we mounted the stairs andlooked down on the packed square. There can be no more Oriental sightthis side of the Atlas and the Sahara. The square is surrounded by lowmud-houses, fondaks, cafés, and the like. In one corner, near thearchway leading into the *souks*, is the fruit-market, where thered-gold branches of unripe dates for animal fodder are piled up ingreat stacks, and dozens of donkeys are coming and going, theirpanniers laden with fruits and vegetables which are being heaped on theground in gorgeous pyramids: purple egg-plants, melons, cucumbers,bright orange pumpkins, mauve and pink and violet onions, rusty crimsonpomegranates and the gold grapes of Sefrou and Salé, all mingled withfresh green sheaves of mint and wormwood.

In the middle of the square sit the story-tellers' turbaned audiences.Beyond these are the humbler crowds about the wild-ringletedsnake-charmers with their epileptic gestures and hissing incantations,and farther off, in the densest circle of all, we could just discern theshaved heads and waving surpliced arms of the dancing-boys. Under anarchway near by an important personage in white muslin, mounted on ahandsome mule and surrounded by his attendants, sat with motionless faceand narrowed eyes gravely following the movements of the dancers.

Suddenly, as we stood watching the extraordinary animation of the scene,a reddish light overspread it, and one of our companions exclaimed:"Ah—a dust-storm!"

In that very moment it was upon us: a red cloud rushing across thesquare out of nowhere, whirling the date-branches over the heads of thesquatting throngs, tumbling down the stacks of fruits and vegetables,rooting up the canvas awnings over the lemonade-sellers' stalls andbefore the café doors, huddling the blinded donkeys under the walls ofthe fondak, and stripping to the hips the black slave-girls scuddinghome from the *souks*.

Such a blast would instantly have scattered any western crowd, but "thepatient East" remained undisturbed, rounding its shoulders before thestorm and continuing to follow attentively the motions of the dancersand the turns of the story-tellers. By and bye, however, the gale grewtoo furious, and the spectators were so involved in collapsing tents,eddying date-branches and stampeding mules that the square began toclear, save for the listeners about the most popular story-teller, whocontinued to sit on unmoved. And then, at the height of the storm, theytoo were abruptly scattered by the rush of a cavalcade across thesquare. First came a handsomely dressed man, carrying before him on hispeaked saddle a tiny boy in a gold-embroidered orange caftan, in frontof whom he held an open book; and behind them a train of white-drapedmen on showily harnessed mules, followed by musicians in bright dresses.It was only a Circumcision procession on its way to the mosque; but thedust-enveloped rider in his rich dress, clutching the bewildered childto his breast, looked like some Oriental prince trying to escape withhis son from the fiery embraces of desert Erl-maidens.

As swiftly as it rose the storm subsided, leaving the fruit-market inruins under a sky as clear and innocent as an infant's eye. The Chleuhboys had vanished with the rest, like marionettes swept into a drawer byan impatient child; but presently, toward sunset, we were told that wewere to see them after all, and our hosts led us up to the roof of theCaïd's house.

The city lay stretched before us like one immense terrace circumscribedby palms. The sky was pure blue, verging to turquoise green where theAtlas floated above mist; and facing the celestial snows stood theKoutoubya, red in the sunset.

People were beginning to come out on the roofs: it was the hour ofpeace, of ablutions, of family life on the house-tops. Groups of womenin pale tints and floating veils spoke to each other from terrace toterrace, through the chatter of children and the guttural calls ofbedizened negresses. And presently, on the roof adjoining ours, appearedthe slim dancing-boys with white caftans and hennaed feet.

The three swarthy musicians who accompanied them crossed their lean legson the tiles and set up their throb-throb and thrum-thrum, and on anarrow strip of terrace the youths began their measured steps.

It was a grave static dance, such as David may have performed before theArk; untouched by mirth or folly, as beseemed a dance in that sombreland, and borrowing its magic from its gravity. Even when the pacequickened with the stress of the music the gestures still continued tobe restrained and hieratic; only when, one by one, the performersdetached themselves from the round and knelt before us for the *peseta*it is customary to press on their foreheads, did one see, by themoisture which made the coin adhere, how quick and violent theirmovements had been.

The performance, like all things Oriental, like the life, the patterns,the stories, seemed to have no beginning and no end: it just wentmonotonously and indefatigably on till fate snipped its thread bycalling us away to dinner. And so at last we went down into the dust ofthe streets refreshed by that vision of white youths dancing on thehouse-tops against the gold of a sunset that made them look—in spite ofankle-bracelets and painted eyes—almost as guileless and happy as theround of angels on the roof of Fra Angelico's Nativity.

VI

THE SAADIAN TOMBS

On one of the last days of our stay in Marrakech we were told, almostmysteriously, that permission was to be given us to visit the tombs ofthe Saadian Sultans.

Though Marrakech has been in the hands of the French since 1912, thevery existence of these tombs was unknown to the authorities till 1917.Then the Sultan's government privately informed the Resident Generalthat an unsuspected treasure of Moroccan art was falling into ruin, andafter some hesitation it was agreed that General Lyautey and theDirector of Fine Arts should be admitted to the mosque containing thetombs, on the express condition that the French Government undertook torepair them. While we were at Rabat General Lyautey had described hisvisit to us, and it was at his request that the Sultan authorized us tosee the mosque, to which no travellers had as yet been admitted.

With a good deal of ceremony, and after the customary *pourparlers* withthe great Pasha who controls native affairs at Marrakech, an hour wasfixed for our visit, and we drove through long lanes of mud-huts to alost quarter near the walls. At last we came to a deserted square on oneside of which stands the long low mosque of Mansourah with aturquoise-green minaret embroidered with traceries of sculptured terracotta. Opposite the mosque is a gate in a crumbling wall; and at thisgate the Pasha's Cadi was to meet us with the keys of the mausoleum. Butwe waited in vain. Oriental dilatoriness, or a last secret reluctance toadmit unbelievers to a holy place, had caused the Cadi to forget hisappointment; and we drove away disappointed.

The delay drove us to wondering about these mysterious Saadian Sultans,who, though coming so late in the annals of Morocco, had left at leastone monument said to be worthy of the Merinid tradition. And the tale ofthe Saadians is worth telling.

They came from Arabia to the Draa (the fruitful country south of theGreat Atlas) early in the fifteenth century, when the Merinid empire wasalready near disintegration. Like all previous invaders they preachedthe doctrine of a pure Islamism to the polytheistic and indifferentBerbers, and found a ready hearing because they denounced the evils of adivided empire, and also because the whole of Morocco was in revoltagainst the Christian colonies of

Spain and Portugal, which hadencircled the coast from Ceuta tó Agadir with a chain of fortifiedcounting-houses. To *bouter dehors* the money-making unbeliever was anobject that found adherents from the Rif to the Sahara, and the Saadiancherifs soon rallied a mighty following to their standard. Islam, thoughit never really gave a creed to the Berbers, supplied them with awar-cry as potent to-day as when it first rang across Barbary.

The history of the Saadians is a foreshortened record of that of alltheir predecessors. They overthrew the artistic and luxurious Merinids,and in their turn became artistic and luxurious. Their greatest Sultan,Abou-el-Abbas, surnamed "The Golden," after defeating the Merinids andputting an end to Christian rule in Morocco by the crushing victory ofEl-Ksar (1578), bethought him in his turn of enriching himself andbeautifying his capital, and with this object in view turned hisattention to the black kingdoms of the south.

Senegal and the Soudan, which had been Mohammedan since the eleventhcentury, had attained in the sixteenth century a high degree ofcommercial wealth and artistic civilization. The Sultanate of Timbuctooseems in reality to have been a thriving empire, and if Timbuctoo wasnot the Claude-like vision of Carthaginian palaces which it became inthe tales of imaginative travellers, it apparently had something of themagnificence of Fez and Marrakech.

The Saadian army, after a march of four and a half months across theSahara, conquered the whole black south. Senegal, the Soudan and Bornousubmitted to Abou-el-Abbas, the Sultan of Timbuctoo was dethroned, andthe celebrated negro jurist Ahmed-Baba was brought a prisoner toMarrakech, where his chief sorrow appears to have been for the loss ofhis library of 1,600 volumes—though he declared that, of all thenumerous members of his family, it was he who possessed the smallestnumber of books.

Besides this learned bibliophile, the Sultan Abou-el-Abbas brought backwith him an immense booty, principally of ingots of gold, from which hetook his surname of "The Golden"; and as the result of the expeditionMarrakech was embellished with mosques and palaces for which the Sultanbrought marble from Carrara, paying for it with loaves of sugar from thesugar-cane that the Saadians grew in the Souss.

In spite of these brilliant beginnings the rule of the dynasty was shortand without subsequent interest. Based on a fanatical antagonismagainst the foreigner, and fed by the ever-wakeful hatred of the Moorsfor their Spanish conquerors, it raised ever higher the Chinese walls ofexclusiveness which the more enlightened Almohads and Merinids hadsought to overthrow. Henceforward less and less daylight and fresh airwere to penetrate into the *souks* of Morocco.

The day after our unsuccessful attempt to see the tombs of theseephemeral rulers we received another message, naming an hour for ourvisit; and this time the Pasha's representative was waiting in thearchway. We followed his lead, under the openly mistrustful glances ofthe Arabs who hung about the square, and after picking our way through atwisting land between walls we came out into a filthy nettle-grown spaceagainst the ramparts. At intervals of about thirty feet splendid squaretowers rose from the walls, and facing one of them lay a group ofcrumbling buildings masked behind other ruins.

We were led first into a narrow mosque or praying-chapel, like those ofthe Medersas, with a coffered cedar ceiling resting on four marblecolumns, and traceried walls of unusually beautiful design. From thischapel we passed into the hall of the tombs, a cube about forty feetsquare. Fourteen columns of colored marble sustain a domed ceiling ofgilded cedar, with an exterior deambulatory under a tunnel-vaulting alsoroofed with cedar. The walls are, as usual, of chiselled stucco, aboverevêtements of ceramic mosaic, and between the columns lie the whitemarble cenotaphs of the Saadian Sultans, covered with Arabicinscriptions in the most delicate low-relief. Beyond this centralmausoleum, and balancing the praying-chapel, lies another long narrowchamber, gold-ceilinged also, and containing a few tombs.

It is difficult, in describing the architecture of Morocco, to avoidproducing an impression of monotony. The ground-plan of mosques andMedersas is always practically the same; and the same elements, few innumber and endlessly repeated, make up the materials and the form of theornament. The effect upon the eye is not monotonous, for a patient arthas infinitely varied the combinations of pattern and the juxtapositionsof color; while the depth of undercutting of the stucco, and thetreatment of the bronze doors and of the carved cedar corbels,necessarily varies with the periods which produced them.

But in the Saadian mausoleum a new element has been introduced whichmakes this little monument a thing apart. The marble columns supportingthe roof appear to be unique in Moroccan architecture, and they lendthemselves to a new roof-plan which relates the building rather to thetradition of Venice or Byzantine by way of Kairouan and Cordova.

The late date of the monument precludes any idea of a direct artistictradition. The most probable explanation seems to be that the architectof the mausoleum was familiar with European Renaissance architecture,and saw the beauty to be derived from using precious marbles not merelyas ornament, but in the Roman and Italian way, as a structural element.Panels and fountain-basins are ornament, and ornament changes nothingessential in architecture; but when, for instance, heavy square piersare replaced by detached columns, a new style results.

It is not only the novelty of its plan that makes the Saadian mausoleumsingular among Moroccan monuments. The details of its ornament are ofthe most intricate refinement: it seems as though the last graces of theexpiring Merinid art had been gathered up into this rare blossom. Andthe slant of sunlight on lustrous columns, the depths of fretted gold,the dusky ivory of the walls and the pure white of the cenotaphs, soclassic in spareness of ornament and simplicity of design—this subtleharmony of form and color gives to the dim rich chapel an air ofdream-like unreality.

And how can it seem other than a dream? Who can have conceived, in theheart of a savage Saharan camp, the serenity and balance of this hiddenplace? And how came such fragile loveliness to survive, preserving,behind a screen of tumbling walls, of nettles and offal and dead beasts,every curve of its traceries and every cell of its honeycombing?

Such questions inevitably bring one back to the central riddle of themysterious North African civilization: the perpetual flux and theimmovable stability, the barbarous customs and sensuous refinements, theabsence of artistic originality and the gift for regrouping borrowedmotives, the patient and exquisite workmanship and the immediate neglectand degradation of the thing once made.

Revering the dead and camping on their graves, elaborating exquisitemonuments only to abandon and defile them, venerating scholarship andwisdom and living in ignorance and grossness, these gifted races,perpetually struggling to reach some higher level of culture from whichthey have always been swept down by a fresh wave of barbarism, are stillonly a people in the making.

It may be that the political stability which France is helping them toacquire will at last give their higher qualities time for fruition; andwhen one looks at the mausoleum of Marrakech and the Medersas of Fez onefeels that, were the experiment made on artistic grounds alone, it wouldyet be well worth making.

V
HAREMS AND CEREMONIES

I

THE CROWD IN THE STREET

To occidental travellers the most vivid impression produced by a firstcontact with the Near East is the surprise of being in a country wherethe human element increases instead of diminishing the delight of theeye.

After all, then, the intimate harmony between nature and architectureand the human body that is revealed in Greek art was not an artist'scounsel of perfection but an honest rendering of reality: there were,there still are, privileged scenes where the fall of a green-grocer'sdraperies or a milkman's cloak or a beggar's rags are part of thecomposition, distinctly related to it in line and colour, and where thenatural unstudied attitudes of the human body are correspondinglyharmonious, however hum-drum the acts it is engaged in. The discovery,to the traveller returning from the East, robs the most romantic scenesof western Europe of half their charm: in the Piazza of San Marco, inthe market-place of Siena, where at least the robes of the Procuratorsor the gay tights of Pinturicchio's striplings once justified man'spresence among his works, one can see, at first, only the outrageinflicted on beauty by the "plentiful strutting manikins" of the modernworld.

Moroccan crowds are always a feast to the eye. The instinct of skilfuldrapery, the sense of colour (subdued by custom, but breaking out insubtle glimpses under the universal ashy tints) make the humblestassemblage of donkey-men and water-carriers an ever-renewed delight. Butit is only on rare occasions, and in the court ceremonies to which sofew foreigners have had access, that the hidden sumptuousness of thenative life is revealed. Even then, the term sumptuousness may seemill-chosen, since the nomadic nature of African life persists in spiteof palaces and chamberlains and all the elaborate ritual of the Makhzen,and the most pompous rites are likely to end in a dusty gallop of wildtribesmen, and the most princely processions to tail off in a string ofhalf-naked urchins riding bareback on donkeys.

As in all Oriental countries, the contact between prince and beggar,vizier and serf is disconcertingly free and familiar, and one must seethe highest court officials kissing the hem of the Sultan's robe, andhear authentic tales of slaves given by one merchant to another at theend of a convivial evening, to be reminded that nothing is as democraticin appearance as a society of which the whole structure hangs on thewhim of one man.

II
AÏD-EL-KEBIR

In the verandah of the Residence of Rabat I stood looking out betweenposts festooned with gentian-blue ipomeas at the first shimmer of lighton black cypresses and white tobacco-flowers, on the scattered roofs ofthe new town, and the plain stretching away to the Sultan's palaceabove the sea.

We had been told, late the night before, that the Sultan would allowMadame Lyautey, with the three ladies of her party, to be present at thegreat religious rite of the Aïd-el-Kebir (the Sacrifice of the Sheep).The honour was an unprecedented one, a favour probably conceded only atthe last moment: for as a rule no women are admitted to theseceremonies. It was an opportunity not to be missed; and all through theshort stifling night I had lain awake wondering if I should be readyearly enough. Presently the motors assembled, and we set out with theFrench officers in attendance on the Governor's wife.

The Sultan's palace, a large modern building on the familiar Arab lines,lies in a treeless and gardenless waste enclosed by high walls and closeabove the blue Atlantic. We motored past the gates, where the Sultan'sBlack Guard was drawn up, and out to the *msalla*, a sort of commonadjacent to all the Sultan's residences where public ceremonies areusually performed. The sun was already beating down on the great plainthronged with horsemen and with the native population of Rabat onmule-back and foot. Within an open space in the centre of the crowd acanvas palissade dyed with a bold black pattern surrounded the Sultan'stents. The Black Guard, in scarlet tunics and white and green turbans,were drawn up on the edge of the open space, keeping the spectators at adistance; but under the guidance of our companions we penetrated to theedge of the crowd.

The palissade was open on one side, and within it we could see movingabout among the snowy-robed officials a group of men in straight narrowgowns of almond-green, peach-blossom, lilac and pink; they were theSultan's musicians, whose coloured dresses always flower outconspicuously among the white draperies of all the other courtattendants.

In the tent nearest the opening, against a background of embroideredhangings, a circle of majestic turbaned old men squatted placidly onRabat rugs. Presently the circle broke up, there was an agitated comingand going, and some one said: "The Sultan has gone to the tent at theback of the enclosure to kill the sheep."

A sense of the impending solemnity ran through the crowd. The mysteriousrumour which is the Voice of the Bazaar rose about us like the wind in apalm-oasis; the Black Guard fired a salute from an adjoining hillock;the clouds of red dust flung up by wheeling horsemen thickened and thenparted, and a white-robed rider sprang out from the tent of theSacrifice with something red and dripping across his saddle-bow, andgalloped away toward Rabat through the shouting. A little shiver ranover the group of occidental spectators, who knew that the dripping redthing was a sheep with its throat so skilfully slit that, if the omenwere favourable, it would live on through the long race to Rabat andgasp out its agonized life on the tiles of the Mosque.

The Sacrifice of the Sheep, one of the four great Moslem rites, issimply the annual propitiatory offering made by every Mahometan head ofa family, and by the Sultan as such. It is based not on a Koranicinjunction, but on the "Souna" or record of the Prophet's "custom" orusages, which forms an authoritative precedent in Moslem ritual. So fargoes the Moslem exegesis. In reality, of course, the Moslemblood-sacrifice comes, by way of the Semitic ritual, from far beyond andbehind it; and the belief that the Sultan's prosperity for the comingyear depends on the animal's protracted agony seems to relate theceremony to the dark magic so deeply rooted in the mysterious tribespeopling North Africa long ages before the first Phoenician prows hadrounded its coast.

Between the Black Guard and the tents, five or six horses were being led up and down by muscular grooms in snowy tunics. They were handsome animals, as Moroccan horses go, and each of a different colour; and on the bay horse was a red saddle embroidered in gold, on the piebald a saddle of peach-colour and silver, on the chestnut, grass-green encrusted with seed-pearls, on the white mare purple housings, and orange velvet on the grey. The Sultan's band had struck up a shrill hammering and twanging, the salute of the Black Guard continued at intervals, and the caparisoned steeds began to rear and snort and drag back from the cruel Arab bits with their exquisite *niello* incrustations. Some one whispered that these were His Majesty's horses—and that it was never known till he appeared which one he would mount.

Presently the crowd about the tents thickened, and when it divided again there emerged from it a grey horse bearing a motionless figure swathed in blinding white. Marching at the horse's bridle, lean brown grooms in white tunics rhythmically waved long strips of white linen to keep off the flies from the Imperial Presence; and beside the motionless rider, in a line with his horse's flank, rode the Imperial Parasol-bearer, who held above the sovereign's head a great sunshade of bright green velvet. Slowly the grey horse advanced a few yards before the tent; behind rode the court dignitaries, followed by the musicians, who looked, in their bright scant caftans, like the slender music-making angels of a Florentine fresco.

The Sultan, pausing beneath his velvet dome, waited to receive the homage of the assembled tribes. An official, riding forward, drew bridle and called out a name. Instantly there came storming across the plain a wild cavalcade of ·tribesmen, with rifles slung across their shoulders, pistols and cutlasses in their belts, and twists of camel's-hair bound about their turbans. Within a few feet of the Sultan they drew in, their leader uttered a cry and sprang forward, bending to the saddle-bow, and with a great shout the tribe galloped by, each man bowed over his horse's neck as he flew past the hieratic figure on the grey horse.

Again and again this ceremony was repeated, the Sultan advancing a few feet as each new group thundered toward him. There were more than ten thousand horsemen and chieftains from the Atlas and the wilderness, and as the ceremony continued the dust-clouds grew denser and morefiery-golden, till at last the forward-surging lines showed through themlike blurred images in a tarnished mirror.

As the Sultan advanced we followed, abreast of him and facing theoncoming squadrons. The contrast between his motionless figure and thewild waves of cavalry beating against it typified the strange soul ofIslam, with its impetuosity forever culminating in impassiveness. Thesun hung high, a brazen ball in a white sky, darting down metallicshafts on the dust-enveloped plain and the serene white figure under itsumbrella. The fat man with a soft round beard-fringed face, wrapped inspirals of pure white, one plump hand on his embroidered bridle, hisyellow-slippered feet thrust heel-down in big velvet-lined stirrups,became, through sheer immobility, a symbol, a mystery, a God. The humanflux beat against him, dissolved, ebbed away, another spear-crested waveswept up behind it and dissolved in turn; and he sat on, hour afterhour, under the white-hot sky, unconscious of the heat, the dust, thetumult, embodying to the wild factious precipitate hordes a longtradition of serene aloofness.

III

THE IMPERIAL MIRADOR

As the last riders galloped up to do homage we were summoned to ourmotors and driven rapidly to the palace. The Sultan had sent word toMme. Lyautey that the ladies of the Imperial harem would entertain herand her guests while his Majesty received the Resident General, and wehad to hasten back in order not to miss the next act of the spectacle.

We walked across a long court lined with the Black Guard, passed under agateway, and were met by a shabbily dressed negress. Traversing a hotdazzle of polychrome tiles we reached another archway guarded by thechief eunuch, a towering black with the enamelled eyes of a basalt bust.The eunuch delivered us to other negresses, and we entered a labyrinthof inner passages and patios, all murmuring and dripping with water.Passing down long corridors where slaves in dim greyish garmentsflattened themselves against the walls, we caught glimpses of great darkrooms, laundries, pantries, bakeries, kitchens, where savoury thingswere brewing and stewing, and where more negresses, abandoning theirpots and pans, came to peep at us from the threshold. In one corner, ona bench against a wall hung with matting, grey parrots in tall cageswere being fed by a slave.

A narrow staircase mounted to a landing where a princess out of an Arabfairy-tale awaited us. Stepping softly on her embroidered slippers sheled us to the nextlanding, where another golden-slippered being smiledout on us, a little girl this one, blushing and dimpling under ajewelled diadem and pearl-woven braids. On a third landing a thirddamsel appeared, and encircled by the three graces we mounted to thetall *mirador* in the central tower from which we were to look down atthe coming ceremony. One by one, our little guides, kicking off theirgolden shoes, which a slave laid neatly outside the door, led us on softbare feet into the upper chamber of the harem.

It was a large room, enclosed on all sides by a balcony glazed withpanes of brightly-coloured glass. On a gaudy modern Rabat carpet stoodgilt armchairs of florid design and a table bearing a commercial bronzeof the "art goods" variety. Divans with muslin-covered cushions wereranged against the walls and down an adjoining gallery-like apartmentwhich was otherwise furnished only with clocks. The passion for clocksand other mechanical contrivances is common to all unmechanical races,and every chief's palace in North Africa contains a collection oftime-pieces which might be called striking if so many had not ceased togo. But those in the Sultan's harem of Rabat are remarkable for the factthat, while designed on current European models, they are proportionedin size to the Imperial dignity, so that a Dutch "grandfather" becomes awardrobe, and the box-clock of the European mantelpiece a cupboard thathas to be set on the floor. At the end of this avenue of time-pieces aEuropean double-bed with a bright silk quilt covered with Nottinghamlace stood majestically on a carpeted platform.

But for the enchanting glimpses of sea and plain through the lattices ofthe gallery, the apartment of the Sultan's ladies falls far short ofoccidental ideas of elegance. But there was hardly time to think ofthis, for the door of the *mirador* was always opening to let in anotherfairy-tale figure, till at last we were surrounded by a dozen houris,laughing, babbling, taking us by the hand, and putting shy questionswhile they looked at us with caressing eyes. They were all (ourinterpretess whispered) the Sultan's "favourites," round-facedapricot-tinted girls in their teens, with high cheek-bones, full redlips, surprised brown eyes between curved-up Asiatic lids, and littlebrown hands fluttering out like birds from their brocaded sleeves.

In honour of the ceremony, and of Mme. Lyautey's visit, they had put ontheir finest clothes, and their freedom of movement was somewhathampered by their narrow sumptuous gowns, with over-draperies of goldand silver brocade and pale rosy gauze held in by corset-like sashes ofgold tissue of Fez, and the heavy silken cords that looped theirvoluminous sleeves. Above their foreheads the hair was shaven like thatof an Italian fourteenth-century beauty, and only a black line as narrowas a pencilled eyebrow showed through the twist of gauze fastened by ajewelled clasp above the real eye-brows. Over the forehead-jewel rosethe complicated structure of the head-dress. Ropes of black wool wereplaited through the hair, forming, at the back, a double loop that stoodout above the nape like the twin handles of a vase, the upper veiled inairy shot gauzes and fastened with jewelled bands and ornaments. On eachside of the red cheeks other braids were looped over the ears hung withbroad earrings of filigree set with rough pearls and emeralds, or goldhoops and pendants of coral; and an unexpected tulle ruff, like that ofa Watteau shepherdess, framed the round chin above a torrent ofnecklaces, necklaces of amber, coral, baroque pearls, hung withmysterious barbaric amulets and fetiches. As the young things movedabout us on soft hennaed feet the light played on shifting gleams ofgold and silver, blue and violet and apple-green, all harmonized andbemisted by clouds of pink and sky-blue; and through the changing groupcapered a little black picaninny in a caftan of silver-shot purple witha sash of raspberry red.

But presently there was a flutter in the aviary. A fresh pair of*babouches* clicked on the landing, and a young girl, less brilliantlydressed and less brilliant of face than the others, came in on barepainted feet. Her movements were shy and hesitating, her large lipspale, her eye-brows less vividly dark, her head less jewelled. But allthe little humming-birds gathered about her with respectful rustlings asshe advanced toward us leaning on one of the young girls, and holdingout her ringed hand to Mme. Lyautey's curtsey. It was the youngPrincess, the Sultan's legitimate daughter. She examined us with sadeyes, spoke a few compliments through the interpretess, and seatedherself in silence, letting the others sparkle and chatter.

Conversation with the shy Princess was flagging when one of the favourites beckoned us to the balcony. We were told we might push open the painted panes a few inches, but as we did so the butterfly group drew back lest they should be seen looking out on the forbidden world.

Salutes were crashing out again from the direction of the *msalla*: puffs of smoke floated over the slopes like thistle-down. Farther off, a pall of red vapour veiled the gallop of the last horsemen wheeling away toward Rabat. The vapour subsided, and moving out of it we discerned a slow procession. First rode a detachment of the Black Guard, mounted on black horses, and, comically fierce in their British scarlet and Meccan green, a uniform invented at the beginning of the nineteenth century by a retired English army officer. After the Guard came the standard-bearers and the great dignitaries, then the Sultan, still aloof, immovable, as if rapt in the contemplation of his mystic office. More court officials followed, then the bright-gowned musicians on foot, then a confused irrepressible crowd of pilgrims, beggars, saints, mountebanks, and the other small folk of the Bazaar, ending in a line of boys jamming their naked heels into the ribs of world-weary donkeys.

The Sultan rode into the court below us, and Vizier and chamberlains, snowy-white against the scarlet line of the Guards, hurried forward to kiss his draperies, his shoes, his stirrup. Descending from his velvet saddle, still entranced, he paced across the tiles between a double line of white servitors bowing to the ground. White pigeons circled over him like petals loosed from a great orchard, and he disappeared with his retinue under the shadowy arcade of the audience chamber at the back of the court.

At this point one of the favourites called us in from the *mirador*. The door had just opened to admit an elderly woman preceded by a respectful group of girls. From the newcomer's round ruddy face, her short round body, the round hands emerging from her round wrists, an inexplicable majesty emanated; and though she too was less richly arrayed than the favourites she carried her head-dress of striped gauze like a crown.

This impressive old lady was the Sultan's mother. As she held out her plump wrinkled hand to Mme. Lyautey and spoke a few words through the interpretess one felt that at last a painted window of the *mirador* had been broken, and a thought let into the vacuum of the harem. What thought, it would have taken deep insight into the processes of the Arab mind to discover; but its honesty was manifest in the old Empress's voice and smile. Here at last was a woman beyond the trivial dissimulations, the childish cunning, the idle cruelties of the harem. It was not a surprise to be told that she was her son's most trusted adviser, and the chief authority in the palace. If such a woman deceived and intrigued it would be for great purposes and for ends she believed in: the depth of her soul had air and daylight in it, and she would never willingly shut them out.

The Empress Mother chatted for a while with Mme. Lyautey, asking about the Resident General's health, enquiring for news of the war, and saying, with an emotion perceptible even through the unintelligible words: "All is well with Morocco as long as all is well with France." Then she withdrew, and we were summoned again to the *mirador*.

This time it was to see a company of officers in brilliant uniforms advancing at a trot across the plain from Rabat. At sight of the figure that headed them, so slim, erect and young on his splendid chestnut, with a pale blue tunic barred by the wide orange ribbon of the Cherifian Order, salutes pealed forth again from the slope above the palace and the Black Guard presented arms. A moment later General Lyautey and his staff were riding in at the gates below us. On the threshold of the inner court they dismounted, and moving to the other side of our balcony we followed the next stage of the ceremony. The Sultan was still seated in the audience chamber. The court officials still stood drawn up in a snow-white line against the snow-white walls. The great dignitaries advanced across the tiles to greet the General; then they fell aside, and he went forward alone, followed at a little distance by his staff. A third of the way across the court he paused, in accordance with the Moroccan court ceremonial, and bowed in the direction of the arcaded room; a few steps farther he bowed again, and a third time on the threshold of the room. Then French uniforms and Moroccan draperies closed in about him, and all vanished into the shadows of the audience hall.

Our audience too seemed to be over. We had exhausted the limited small talk of the harem, had learned from the young beauties that, though they were forbidden to look on at the ceremony, the dancers and singers would come to entertain them presently, and had begun to take leave when a negress hurried in to say that his Majesty begged Mme. Lyautey and herfriends to await his arrival. This was the crowning incident of ourvisit, and I wondered with what Byzantine ritual the Anointed One freshfrom the exercise of his priestly functions would be received among hiswomen.

The door opened, and without any announcement or other preliminaryflourish a fat man with a pleasant face, his djellabah stretched over aportly front, walked in holding a little boy by the hand. Such was hisMajesty the Sultan Moulay Youssef, despoiled of sacramental burnousesand turban, and shuffling along on bare yellow-slippered feet with thegait of a stout elderly gentleman who has taken off his boots in thepassage preparatory to a domestic evening.

The little Prince, one of his two legitimate sons, was dressed withequal simplicity, for silken garments are worn in Morocco only bymusicians, boy-dancers and other hermaphrodite fry. With his ceremonialraiment the Sultan had put off his air of superhuman majesty, and theexpression of his round pale face corresponded with the plainness of hisdress. The favourites fluttered about him, respectful but by no meansawestruck, and the youngest began to play with the little Prince. Wecould well believe the report that his was the happiest harem inMorocco, as well as the only one into which a breath of the outer worldever came.

Moulay Youssef greeted Mme. Lyautey with friendly simplicity, made theproper speeches to her companions, and then, with the air of thebusiness-man who has forgotten to give an order before leaving hisoffice, he walked up to a corner of the room, and while theflower-maidens ruffled about him, and through the windows we saw thelast participants in the mystic rites galloping away toward thecrenellated walls of Rabat, his Majesty the Priest and Emperor of theFaithful unhooked a small instrument from the wall and applied hissacred lips to the telephone.

IV

IN OLD RABAT

Before General Lyautey came to Morocco Rabat had been subjected to theindignity of European "improvements," and one must traverse boulevardsscored with tram-lines, and pass between hotel-terraces and cafés andcinema-palaces, to reach the surviving nucleus of the once beautifulnative town. Then, at the turn of a commonplace street, one comes uponit suddenly. The shops and cafés cease, the jingle of trams and thetrumpeting of motor-horns die out, and here, all at once, are silenceand solitude, and the dignified reticence of the windowless Arabhouse-fronts.

We were bound for the house of a high government official, a Moroccandignitary of the old school, who had invited us to tea, and added amessage to the effect that the ladies of his household would be happy toreceive me.

The house we sought was some distance down the quietest of white-walledstreets. Our companion knocked at a low green door, and we were admittedto a passage into which a wooden stairway descended. A brother-in-law ofour host was waiting for us: in his wake we mounted the ladder-likestairs and entered a long room with a florid French carpet and a set ofgilt furniture to match. There were no fretted walls, no painted cedardoors, no fountains rustling in unseen courts: the house was squeezed inbetween others, and such traces of old ornament as it may have possessedhad vanished.

But presently we saw why its inhabitants were indifferent to suchdetails. Our host, a handsome white-bearded old man, welcomed us in thedoorway; then he led us to a raised oriel window at one end of the room,and seated us in the gilt armchairs face to face with one of the mostbeautiful views in Morocco.

Below us lay the white and blue terrace-roofs of the native town, withpalms and minarets shooting up between them, or the shadows of avine-trellis patterning a quiet lane. Beyond, the Atlantic sparkled,breaking into foam at the mouth of the Bou-Regreg and under the toweringramparts of the Kasbah of the Oudayas. To the right, the ruins of thegreat Mosque rose from their plateau over the river; and, on the fartherside of the troubled flood, old Salé, white and wicked, lay like a jewelin its gardens. With such a scene beneath their eyes, the inhabitants ofthe house could hardly feel its lack of architectural interest.

After exchanging the usual compliments, and giving us time to enjoy theview, our host withdrew, taking with him the men of our party. A momentlater he reappeared with a rosy fair-haired girl, dressed in Arabcostume, but evidently of European birth. The brother-in-law explainedthat this young woman, who had "studied in Algeria," and whose motherwas French, was the intimate friend of the ladies of the household, andwould act as interpreter. Our host then again left us, joining the menvisitors in another room, and the door opened to admit his wife anddaughters-in-law.

The mistress of the house was a handsome Algerian with sad expressiveeyes: the younger women were pale, fat and amiable. They all wore soberdresses, in keeping with the simplicity of the house, and but for thevacuity of their faces the group might have been that of a Professor'sfamily in an English or American University town, decently costumed foran Arabian Nights' pageant in the college grounds. I was never morevividly reminded of the fact that human nature, from one pole to theother, falls naturally into certain categories, and that Respectabilitywears the same face in an Oriental harem as in England or America.

My hostesses received me with the utmost amiability, we seated ourselvesin the oriel facing the view, and the interchange of questions andcompliments began.

Had I any children? (They asked it all at once.)

Alas, no.

"In Islam" (one of the ladies ventured) "a woman without children isconsidered the most unhappy being in the world."

I replied that in the western world also childless women were pitied.(The brother-in-law smiled incredulously.)

Knowing that European fashions are of absorbing interest to the harem Inext enquired: "What do these ladies think of our stiff tailor-dresses?Don't they find them excessively ugly?"

"Yes, they do;" (it was again the brother-in-law who replied.) "But theysuppose that in your own homes you dress less badly."

"And have they never any desire to travel, or to visit the Bazaars, asthe Turkish ladies do?"

"No, indeed. They are too busy to give such matters a thought. In ourcountry women of the highest class occupy themselves with theirhousehold and their children, and the rest of their time is devoted toneedlework." (At this statement I gave the brother-in-law a smile asincredulous as his own.)

All this time the fair-haired interpretess had not been allowed by thevigilant guardian of the harem to utter a word.

I turned to her with a question.

"So your mother is French, *Mademoiselle?*"

"*Oui, Madame.*"

"From what part of France did she come?"

A bewildered pause. Finally: "I don't know ... from Switzerland, I think," brought out this shining example of the Higher Education. In spite of Algerian "advantages" the poor girl could speak only a few words of her mother's tongue. She had kept the European features and complexion, but her soul was the soul of Islam. The harem had placed its powerful imprint upon her, and she looked at me with the same remote and passive eyes as the daughters of the house.

After struggling for a while longer with a conversation which the watchful brother-in-law continued to direct as he pleased. I felt my own lips stiffening into the resigned smile of the harem, and it was a relief when at last their guardian drove the pale flock away, and the handsome old gentleman who owned them reappeared on the scene, bringing back my friends, and followed by slaves and tea.

V

IN FEZ

What thoughts, what speculations, one wonders, go on under the narrow veiled brows of the little creatures destined to the high honour of marriage or concubinage in Moroccan palaces?

Some are brought down from mountains and cedar forests, from the free life of the tents where the nomad women go unveiled. Others come from harems in the turreted cities beyond the Atlas, where blue palm-groves beat all night against the stars and date-caravans journey across the desert from Timbuctoo. Some, born and bred in an airy palace among pomegranate gardens and white terraces, pass thence to one of the feudal fortresses near the snows, where for half the year the great chiefs of the south live in their clan, among fighting men and falconers and packs of *sloughis*. And still others grow up in a stifling Mellah, trip unveiled on its blue terraces overlooking the gardens of the great, and, seen one day at sunset by a fat vizier or his pale young master, are acquired for a handsome sum and transferred to the painted sepulchre of the harem.

Worst of all must be the fate of those who go from tents and cedarforests, or from some sea-blown garden above Rabat, into one of thehouses of Old Fez. They are well-nigh impenetrable, these palaces ofElbali: the Fazi dignitaries do not welcome the visits of strange women.On the rare occasions when they are received, a member of the family(one of the sons, or a brother-in-law who has "studied in Algeria")usually acts as interpreter; and perhaps it is as well that no one fromthe outer world should come to remind these listless creatures thatsomewhere the gulls dance on the Atlantic and the wind murmurs througholive-yards and clatters the metallic fronds of palm-groves.

We had been invited, one day, to visit the harem of one of the chiefdignitaries of the Makhzen at Fez, and these thoughts came to me as Isat among the pale women in their mouldering prison. The descent throughthe steep tunnelled streets gave one the sense of being lowered into theshaft of a mine. At each step the strip of sky grew narrower, and wasmore often obscured by the low vaulted passages into which we plunged.The noises of the Bazaar had died out, and only the sound of fountainsbehind garden walls and the clatter of our mules' hoofs on the stoneswent with us. Then fountains and gardens ceased also, the toweringmasonry closed in, and we entered an almost subterranean labyrinth whichsun and air never reach. At length our mules turned into a *cul-de-sac*blocked by a high building. On the right was another building, one ofthose blind mysterious house-fronts of Fez that seem like a fragment ofits ancient fortifications. Clients and servants lounged on the stonebenches built into the wall; it was evidently the house of an importantperson. A charming youth with intelligent eyes waited on the thresholdto receive us: he was one of the sons of the house, the one who had"studied in Algeria" and knew how to talk to visitors. We followed himinto a small arcaded *patio* hemmed in by the high walls of the house.On the right was the usual long room with archways giving on the court.Our host, a patriarchal personage, draped in fat as in a toga, cametoward us, a mountain of majestic muslins, his eyes sparkling in aswarthy silver-bearded face. He seated us on divans and lowered hisvoluminous person to a heap of cushions on the step leading into thecourt; and the son who had studied in Algeria instructed a negress toprepare the tea.

Across the *patio* was another arcade closely hung with unbleachedcotton. From behind it came the sound of chatter, and now and then abare brown child in a scant shirt would escape, and be hurriedly pulledback with soft explosions of laughter, while a black woman came out toreadjust the curtains.

There were three of these negresses, splendid bronze creatures, wearingwhite djellabahs over bright-coloured caftans, striped scarves knottedabout their large hips, and gauze turbans on their crinkled hair. Theirwrists clinked with heavy silver bracelets, and big circular earringsdanced in their purple ear-lobes. A languor lay on all the other inmatesof the household, on the servants and hangers-on squatting in the shadeunder the arcade, on our monumental host and his smiling son; but thethree negresses, vibrating with activity, rushed continually from thecurtained chamber to the kitchen, and from the kitchen to the master'sreception-room, bearing on their pinky-blue palms trays of Britanniametal with tall glasses and fresh bunches of mint, shouting orders todozing menials, and calling to each other from opposite ends of thecourt; and finally the stoutest of the three, disappearing from view,reappeared suddenly on a pale green balcony overhead, where, profiledagainst a square of blue sky, she leaned over in a Veronese attitude andscreamed down to the others like an excited parrot.

In spite of their febrile activity and tropical bird-shrieks, we waitedin vain for tea; and after a while our host suggested to his son that Imight like to visit the ladies of the household. As I had expected, theyoung man led me across the *patio*, lifted the cotton hanging andintroduced me into an apartment exactly like the one we had just left.Divans covered with striped mattress-ticking stood against the whitewalls, and on them sat seven or eight passive-looking women over whom anumber of pale children scrambled.

The eldest of the group, and evidently the mistress of the house,was an Algerian lady, probably of about fifty, with a sad anddelicately-modelled face; the others were daughters, daughters-in-lawand concubines. The latter word evokes to occidental ears images ofsensual seduction which the Moroccan harem seldom realizes. All theladies of this dignified official household wore the same look ofsomewhat melancholy respectability. In their stuffy curtained apartmentthey were like cellar-grown flowers, pale, heavy, fuller but frailerthan the garden sort. Their dresses, rich but sober, the veils anddiadems put on in honour of my visit, had a dignified dowdiness in oddcontrast to the frivolity of the Imperial harem. But what chiefly struckme was the apathy of the younger women. I asked them if they had agarden, and they shook their heads wistfully, saying that there were nogardens in Old Fez. The roof was therefore their only escape: a roofoverlooking acres and acres of other roofs, and closed in by the nakedfortified mountains which stand about Fez like prison-walls.

After a brief exchange of compliments silence fell. Conversing throughinterpreters is a benumbing process, and there are few points of contactbetween the open-air occidental mind and beings imprisoned in aconception of sexual and domestic life based on slave-service andincessant espionage. These languid women on their muslin cushions toilnot, neither do they spin. The Moroccan lady knows little of cooking,needlework or any household arts. When her child is ill she can onlyhang it with amulets and wail over it; the great lady of the Fazi palaceis as ignorant of hygiene as the peasant-woman of the *bled*. And allthese colourless eventless lives depend on the favour of one fattyrannical man, bloated with good living and authority, himself almostas inert and sedentary as his women, and accustomed to impose his whimson them ever since he ran about the same *patio* as a littleshort-smocked boy.

The redeeming point in this stagnant domesticity is the tenderness ofthe parents for their children, and western writers have laid so muchstress on this that one would suppose children could be loved only byinert and ignorant parents. It is in fact charming to see the heavy eyesof the Moroccan father light up when a brown grasshopper baby jumps onhis knee, and the unfeigned tenderness with which the childless women ofthe harem caress the babies of their happier rivals. But thesentimentalist moved by this display of family feeling would do well toconsider the lives of these much-petted children. Ignorance,unhealthiness and a precocious sexual initiation prevail in all classes.Education consists in learning by heart endless passages of the Koran,and amusement in assisting at spectacles that would be unintelligibleto western children, but that the pleasantries of the harem makeperfectly comprehensible to Moroccan infancy. At eight or nine thelittle girls are married, at twelve the son of the house is "given hisfirst negress"; and thereafter, in the rich and leisured class, bothsexes live till old age in an atmosphere of sensuality withoutseduction.

The young son of the house led me back across the court, where thenegresses were still shrieking and scurrying, and passing to and frolike a stage-procession with the vain paraphernalia of a tea that nevercame. Our host still smiled from his cushions, resigned to Orientaldelays. To distract the impatient westerners, a servant unhooked fromthe wall the cage of a gently-cooing dove. It was brought to us, stillcooing, and looked at me with the same resigned and vacant eyes as theladies I had just left. As it was being restored to its hook the slaveslolling about the entrance scattered respectfully at the approach of ahandsome man of about thirty, with delicate features and a black beard.Crossing the court, he stooped to kiss the shoulder of our host, whointroduced him as his eldest son, the husband of one or two of thelittle pale wives with whom I had been exchanging platitudes.

From the increasing agitation of the negresses it became evident thatthe ceremony of tea-making had been postponed till his arrival. A metaltray bearing a Britannia samovar and tea-pot was placed on the tiles ofthe court, and squatting beside it the newcomer gravely proceeded toinfuse the mint. Suddenly the cotton hangings fluttered again, and atiny child in the scantest of smocks rushed out and scampered across thecourt. Our venerable host, stretching out rapturous arms, caught thefugitive to his bosom, where the little boy lay like a squirrel,watching us with great sidelong eyes. He was the last-born of thepatriarch, and the youngest brother of the majestic bearded gentlemanengaged in tea-making. While he was still in his father's arms two moresons appeared: charming almond-eyed schoolboys returning from theirKoran-class, escorted by their slaves. All the sons greeted each otheraffectionately, and caressed with almost feminine tenderness the dancingbaby so lately added to their ranks; and finally, to crown this scene ofdomestic intimacy, the three negresses, their gigantic effort at lastaccomplished, passed about glasses of steaming mint and trays ofgazelles' horns and white sugar-cakes.

VI

IN MARRAKECH

The farther one travels from the Mediterranean and Europe the closer thecurtains of the women's quarters are drawn. The only harem in which wewere allowed an interpreter was that of the Sultan himself; in theprivate harems of Fez and Rabat a French-speaking relative transmitted(or professed to transmit) our remarks; in Marrakech, the great noblemanand dignitary who kindly invited me to visit his household was deaf toour hint that the presence of a lady from one of the French governmentschools might facilitate our intercourse.

When we drove up to his palace, one of the stateliest in Marrakech, thestreet was thronged with clansmen and clients. Dignified merchants inwhite muslin, whose grooms held white mules saddled with rose-colouredvelvet, warriors from the Atlas wearing the corkscrew ringlets which area sign of military prowess, Jewish traders in black gabardines,leather-gaitered peasant-women with chickens and cheese, and beggarsrolling their blind eyes or exposing their fly-plastered sores, weregathered in Oriental promiscuity about the great man's door; while underthe archway stood a group of youths and warlike-looking older men whowere evidently of his own clan.

The Caïd's chamberlain, a middle-aged man of dignified appearance,advanced to meet us between bowing clients and tradesmen. He led usthrough cool passages lined with the intricate mosaic-work of Fez, pastbeggars who sat on stone benches whining out their blessings, and paleFazi craftsmen laying a floor of delicate tiles. The Caïd is a lover ofold Arab architecture. His splendid house, which is not yet finished,has been planned and decorated on the lines of the old Imperial palaces,and when a few years of sun and rain and Oriental neglect have workedtheir way on its cedar-wood and gilding and ivory stucco it will havethe same faded loveliness as the fairy palaces of Fez.

In a garden where fountains splashed and roses climbed among cypresses,the Caïd himself awaited us. This great fighter and loyal friend ofFrance is a magnificent eagle-beaked man, brown, lean and sinewy, withvigilant eyes looking out under his carefully draped muslin turban, andnegroid lips half-hidden by a close black beard.

Tea was prepared in the familiar setting; a long arcaded room withpainted ceiling and richly stuccoed walls. All around were ranged theusual mattresses covered with striped ticking and piled with muslincushions. A bedstead of brass, imitating a Louis XVI cane bed, andadorned with brass garlands and bows, throned on the usual platform; andthe only other ornaments were a few clocks and bunches of wax flowersunder glass. Like all Orientals, this hero of the Atlas, who spends halfhis life with his fighting clansmen in a mediæval stronghold among thesnows, and the other half rolling in a 60 h.p. motor over smooth Frenchroads, seems unaware of any degrees of beauty or appropriateness inobjects of European design, and places against the exquisite mosaicsand traceries of his Fazi craftsmen the tawdriest bric-à-brac of thecheap department-store.

While tea was being served I noticed a tiny negress, not more than sixor seven years old, who stood motionless in the embrasure of an archway.Like most of the Moroccan slaves, even in the greatest households, shewas shabbily, almost raggedly, dressed. A dirty *gandourah* of stripedmuslin covered her faded caftan, and a cheap kerchief was wound aboveher grave and precocious little face. With preternatural vigilance shewatched each movement of the Caïd, who never spoke to her, looked ather, or made her the slightest perceptible sign, but whose least wishshe instantly divined, refilling his tea-cup, passing the plates ofsweets, or removing our empty glasses, in obedience to some secrettelegraphy on which her whole being hung.

The Caïd is a great man. He and his famous elder brother, holding thesouthern marches of Morocco against alien enemies and internalrebellion, played a preponderant part in the defence of the Frenchcolonies in North Africa during the long struggle of the war.Enlightened, cultivated, a friend of the arts, a scholar anddiplomatist, he seems, unlike many Orientals, to have selected the bestin assimilating European influences. Yet when I looked at the tinycreature watching him with those anxious joyless eyes I felt once morethe abyss that slavery and the seraglio put between the mostEuropeanized Mahometan and the western conception of life. The Caïd'slittle black slaves are well-known in Morocco, and behind the sad childleaning in the archway stood all the shadowy evils of the social systemthat hangs like a millstone about the neck of Islam.

Presently a handsome tattered negress came across the garden to invite me to the harem. Captain de S. and his wife, who had accompanied me, were old friends of the Chief's, and it was owing to this that the jealously-guarded doors of the women's quarters were opened to Mme de S. and myself. We followed the negress to a marble-paved court where pigeons fluttered and strutted about the central fountain. From under a trellised arcade hung with linen curtains several ladies came forward. They greeted my companion with exclamations of delight; then they led us into the usual commonplace room with divans and whitewashed walls. Even in the most sumptuous Moroccan palaces little care seems to be expended on the fittings of the women's quarters: unless, indeed, the room in which visitors are received corresponds with a boarding-school "parlour," and the personal touch is reserved for the private apartments.

The ladies who greeted us were more richly dressed than any I had seen except the Sultan's favourites; but their faces were more distinguished, more European in outline, than those of the round-cheeked beauties of Rabat. My companions had told me that the Caïd's harem was recruited from Georgia, and that the ladies receiving us had been brought up in the relative freedom of life in Constantinople; and it was easy to read in their wistfully smiling eyes memories of a life unknown to the passive daughters of Morocco.

They appeared to make no secret of their regrets, for presently one of them, with a smile, called my attention to some faded photographs hanging over the divan. They represented groups of plump provincial-looking young women in dowdy European ball-dresses; and it required an effort of the imagination to believe that the lovely creatures in velvet caftans, with delicately tattooed temples under complicated head-dresses, and hennaed feet crossed on muslin cushions, were the same as the beaming frumps in the photographs. But to the sumptuously-clad exiles these faded photographs and ugly dresses represented freedom, happiness, and all they had forfeited when fate (probably in the shape of an opulent Hebrew couple "travelling with their daughters") carried them from the Bosphorus to the Atlas.

As in the other harems I had visited, perfect equality seemed to prevail between the ladies, and while they chatted with Mme de S. whose few words of Arabic had loosed their tongues, I tried to guess which was thefavourite, or at least the first in rank. My choice wavered between thepretty pale creature with a *ferronnière* across her temples and atea-rose caftan veiled in blue gauze, and the nut-brown beauty in redvelvet hung with pearls whose languid attitudes and long-lidded eyeswere so like the Keepsake portraits of Byron's Haïdee. Or was it perhapsthe third, less pretty but more vivid and animated, who sat behind thetea-tray, and mimicked so expressively a soldier shouldering his rifle,and another falling dead, in her effort to ask us "when the dreadful warwould be over"? Perhaps ... unless, indeed, it were the handsomeoctoroon, slightly older than the others, but even more richly dressed,so free and noble in her movements, and treated by the others with suchfriendly deference.

I was struck by the fact that among them all there was not a child; itwas the first harem without babies that I had seen in that prolificland. Presently one of the ladies asked Mme. de S. about her children;in reply, she enquired for the Caïd's little boy, the son of his wifewho had died. The ladies' faces lit up wistfully, a slave was given anorder, and presently a large-eyed ghost of a child was brought into theroom.

Instantly all the bracelet-laden arms were held out to the dead woman'sson; and as I watched the weak little body hung with amulets and theheavy head covered with thin curls pressed against a brocaded bosom, Iwas reminded of one of the coral-hung child-Christs of Crivelli,standing livid and waxen on the knee of a splendidly dressed Madonna.

The poor baby on whom such hopes and ambitions hung stared at us with asolemn unamused gaze. Would all his pretty mothers, his eyes seemed toask, succeed in bringing him to maturity in spite of the parched summersof the south and the stifling existence of the harem? It was evidentthat no precaution had been neglected to protect him from maleficentinfluences and the danger that walks by night, for his frail neck andwrists were hung with innumerable charms: Koranic verses, Soudaneseincantations, and images of forgotten idols in amber and coral and hornand ambergris. Perhaps they will ward off the powers of evil, and lethim grow up to shoulder the burden of the great Caïds of the south.

VI
GENERAL LYAUTEY'S WORK IN MOROCCO

I

It is not too much to say that General Lyautey has twice saved Moroccofrom destruction: once in 1912, when the inertia and double-dealing ofAbd-el-Hafid abandoned the country to the rebellious tribes who hadattacked him in Fez, and the second time in August, 1914, when Germanydeclared war on France.

In 1912, in consequence of the threatening attitude of the dissidenttribes and the generally disturbed condition of the country, the SultanAbd-el-Hafid had asked France to establish a protectorate in Morocco.The agreement entered into, called the "Convention of Fez," stipulatedthat a French Resident-General should be sent to Morocco with authorityto act as the Sultan's sole representative in treating with the otherpowers. The convention was signed in March, 1912, and a few daysafterward an uprising more serious than any that had gone before tookplace in Fez. This sudden outbreak was due in part to purely local andnative difficulties, in part to the intrinsic weakness of the Frenchsituation. The French government had imagined that a native armycommanded by French officers could be counted on to support the Makhzenand maintain order; but Abd-el-Hafid's growing unpopularity hadestranged his own people from him, and the army turned on the governmentand on the French. On the 17th of April, 1912, the Moroccan soldiersmassacred their French officers after inflicting horrible tortures onthem; the population of Fez rose against the European civilians, and fora fortnight the Oued Fez ran red with the blood of harmless Frenchcolonists. It was then that France appointed General LyauteyResident-General in Morocco.

When he reached Fez it was besieged by twenty thousand Berbers. Rebeltribes were flocking in to their support, to the cry of the Holy War;and the terrified Sultan, who had already announced his intention ofresigning, warned the French troops who were trying to protect him thatunless they guaranteed to get him safely to Rabat he would turn hisinfluence against them. Two days afterward the Berbers attacked Fez andbroke in at two gates. The French drove them out and forced them backtwenty miles. The outskirts of the city were rapidly fortified, and afew weeks later General Gouraud, attacking the rebels in the valley ofthe Sebou, completely disengaged Fez.

The military danger overcome, General Lyautey began his great task ofcivilian administration. His aim was to support and strengthen theexisting government, to reassure and pacify the distrustful andantagonistic elements, and to assert French authority without irritatingor discouraging native ambitions.

Meanwhile a new Mahdi (Ahmed-el-Hiba) had risen in the south.Treacherously supported by Abd-el-Hafid, he was proclaimed Sultan atTiznit, and acknowledged by the whole of the Souss. In Marrakech, nativeunrest had caused the Europeans to fly to the coast, and in the north anew group of rebellious tribes menaced Fez.

El-Hiba entered Marrakech in August, 1912, and the French consul andseveral other French residents were taken prisoner. El-Hiba's forcesthen advanced to a point half way between Marrakech and Mazagan, whereGeneral Mangin, at that time a colonial colonel, met and utterly routedthem. The disorder in the south, and the appeals of the nativepopulation for protection against the savage depredations of the newMahdist rebels, made it necessary for the French troops to follow uptheir success; and in September Marrakech was taken.

Such were the swift and brilliant results of General Lyautey'sintervention. The first difficulties had been quickly overcome; others,far more complicated, remained. The military occupation of Morocco hadto be followed up by its civil reorganization. By the Franco-Germantreaty of 1911 Germany had finally agreed to recognize the Frenchprotectorate in Morocco; but in spite of an apparently explicitacknowledgment of this right, Germany, as usual, managed to slip intothe contract certain ambiguities of form that were likely to lead tofuture trouble.

To obtain even this incomplete treaty France had had to sacrifice partof her colonies in equatorial Africa; and in addition to the uncertainrelation with Germany there remained the dead weight of the Spanish zoneand the confused international administration of Tangier. Thedisastrously misgoverned Spanish zone has always been a centre forGerman intrigue and native conspiracies, as well as a permanent obstacleto the economic development of Morocco.

Such were the problems that General Lyautey found awaiting him. A longcolonial experience, and an unusual combination of military andadministrative talents, prepared him for the almost impossible task ofdealing with them. Swift and decisive when military action is required,he has above all the long views and endless patience necessary to thesuccessful colonial governor. The policy of France in Morocco has beenweak and spasmodic; in his hands it became firm and consecutive. Asympathetic understanding of the native prejudices, and a real affectionfor the native character, made him try to build up an administrationwhich should be, not an application of French ideas to Africanconditions, but a development of the best native aspirations. Thedifficulties were immense. The attempt to govern as far as possiblethrough the Great Chiefs was a wise one; but it was hampered by the factthat these powerful leaders, however loyal to the Protectorate, knew nomethods of administration but .those based on extortion. It was necessaryat once to use them and to educate them; and one of General Lyautey'sgreatest achievements has been the successful employment of nativeability in the government of the country.

II

The first thing to do was to create a strong frontier against thedissident tribes of the Blad-es-Siba. To do this it was necessary thatthe French should hold the natural defenses of the country, thefoothills of the Little and of the Great Atlas, and the valley of theMoulouya, which forms the corridor between western Algeria and Morocco.This was nearly accomplished in 1914 when war broke out.

At that moment the home government cabled the Resident-General to sendall his available troops to France, abandoning the whole of conqueredterritory except the coast towns. To do so would have been to giveFrance's richest colonies outright to Germany at a moment when whatthey could supply—meat and wheat—was exactly what the enemy mostneeded.

General Lyautey took forty-eight hours to consider. He then decided to"empty the egg without breaking the shell"; and the reply he sent wasthat of a great patriot and a great general. In effect he said: "I willgive you all the troops you ask, but instead of abandoning the interiorof the country I will hold what we have already taken, and fortify andenlarge our boundaries." No other military document has so nearly thatring as Marshal Foch's immortal Marne despatch (written only a few weekslater): "My centre is broken, my right wing is wavering, the situationis favorable and I am about to attack."

General Lyautey had framed his answer in a moment of patrioticexaltation, when the soul of every Frenchman was strung up to asuperhuman pitch. But the pledge once made, it had to be carried out;and even those who most applauded his decision wondered how he wouldmeet the almost insuperable difficulties it involved. Morocco, when hewas called there, was already honey-combed by German trading interestsand secret political intrigue, and the fruit seemed ready to fall whenthe declaration of war shook the bough. The only way to save the colonyfor France was to keep its industrial and agricultural life going, andgive to the famous "business as usual" a really justifiable application.

General Lyautey completely succeeded, and the first impression of alltravellers arriving in Morocco two years later was that of suddenlyreturning to a world in normal conditions. There was even, so completewas the illusion, a first moment of almost painful surprise on enteringan active prosperous community, seemingly absorbed in immediate materialinterests to the exclusion of all thought of the awful drama that wasbeing played out in the mother country; and it was only on reflectionthat this absorption in the day's task, and this air of smiling faithin the future, were seen to be Morocco's truest way of serving France.

For not only was France to be supplied with provisions, but theconfidence in her ultimate triumph was at all costs to be kept up in thenative mind. German influence was as deep-seated as a cancer: to cut itout required the most drastic of operations. And that operationconsisted precisely in letting it be seen that France was strong andprosperous enough for her colonies to thrive and expand without fearwhile she held at bay on her own frontier the most formidable foe theworld has ever seen. Such was the "policy of the smile," consistentlyadvocated by General Lyautey from the beginning of the war, and of whichhe and his household were the first to set the example.

III

The General had said that he would not "break the egg-shell"; but heknew that this was not enough, and that he must make it appearunbreakable if he were to retain the confidence of the natives.

How this was achieved, with the aid of the few covering troops left him,is still almost incomprehensible. To hold the line was virtuallyimpossible: therefore he pushed it forward. An anonymous writer in*L'Afrique Française* (January, 1917) has thus described themanoeuvre: "General Henrys was instructed to watch for storm-signalson the front, to stop up the cracks, to strengthen weak points and torectify doubtful lines. Thanks to these operations, which kept therebels perpetually harassed by always forestalling their own plans, theoccupied territory was enlarged by a succession of strongly fortifiedpositions." While this was going on in the north, General Lamothe wasextending and strengthening, by means of pacific negotiations, theinfluence of the Great Chiefs in the south; and other agents of theResidency were engaged in watching and thwarting the incessant Germanintrigues in the Spanish zone.

General Lyautey is quoted as having said that "a work-shop is worth abattalion." This precept he managed to put into action even during thefirst dark days of 1914, and the interior development of Moroccoproceeded side by side with the strengthening of its defenses. Germanyhad long foreseen what an asset northwest Africa would be during thewar; and General Lyautey was determined to prove how right Germany hadbeen. He did so by getting the government, to whom he had given nearlyall his troops, to give him in exchange an agricultural and industrialarmy, or at least enough specialists to form such an army out of theavailable material in the country. For every battle fought a road wasmade; for every rebel fortress shelled a factory was built, a harbordeveloped, or more miles of fallow land ploughed and sown.

But this economic development did not satisfy the Resident. He wishedMorocco to enlarge her commercial relations with France and the otherallied countries, and with this object in view he organized and carriedout with brilliant success a series of exhibitions at Casablanca, Fezand

Rabat. The result of this bold policy surpassed even its creator'shopes. The Moroccans of the plain are an industrious and money-lovingpeople, and the sight of these rapidly improvised exhibitions, where theindustrial and artistic products of France and other European countrieswere shown in picturesque buildings grouped about flower-filled gardens,fascinated their imagination and strengthened their confidence in thecountry that could find time for such an effort in the midst of a greatwar. The Voice of the Bazaar carried the report to the farthest confinesof Moghreb, and one by one the notabilities of the different tribesarrived, with delegations from Algeria and Tunisia. It was even saidthat several rebel chiefs had submitted to the Makhzen in order not tomiss the Exhibition.

At the same time as the "Miracle of the Marne" another, less famous butalmost as vital to France, was being silently performed at the otherend of her dominions. It will not seem an exaggeration to speak ofGeneral Lyautey's achievement during the first year of the war as the"Miracle of Morocco" if one considers the immense importance of doingwhat he did at the moment when he did it. And to understand this it isonly needful to reckon what Germany could have drawn in supplies and menfrom a German North Africa, and what would have been the situation ofFrance during the war with a powerful German colony in control of thewestern Mediterranean.

General Lyautey has always been one of the clear-sighted administratorswho understand that the successful government of a foreign countrydepends on many little things, and not least on the administrator'sgenuine sympathy with the traditions, habits and tastes of the people. Akeen feeling for beauty had prepared him to appreciate all that was mostexquisite and venerable in the Arab art of Morocco, and even in thefirst struggle with political and military problems he found time togather about him a group of archæologists and artists who were chargedwith the inspection and preservation of the national monuments and therevival of the languishing native art-industries. The old pottery,jewelry, metal-work, rugs and embroideries of the different regions werecarefully collected and classified; schools of decorative art werefounded, skilled artisans sought out, and every effort was made to urgeEuropean residents to follow native models and use native artisans inbuilding and furnishing.

At the various Exhibitions much space was allotted to these revivedindustries, and the matting of Salé, the rugs of Rabat, the embroideriesof Fez and Marrakech have already found a ready market in France,besides awakening in the educated class of colonists an appreciation ofthe old buildings and the old arts of the country that will be itssurest safeguard against the destructive effects of colonial expansion.It is only necessary to see the havoc wrought in Tunisia and Algeria bythe heavy hand of the colonial government to know what General Lyauteyhas achieved in saving Morocco from this form of destruction, also.

All this has been accomplished by the Resident-General during five yearsof unexampled and incessant difficulty; and probably the trueexplanation of the miracle is that which he himself gives when he says,with the quiet smile that typifies his Moroccan war-policy: "It was easyto do because I loved the people."

THE WORK OF THE FRENCH PROTECTORATE, 1912-1918
PORTS

Owing to the fact that the neglected and roadless Spanish zoneintervened between the French possessions and Tangier, which is thenatural port of Morocco, one of the first pre-occupations of GeneralLyautey was to make ports along the inhospitable Atlantic coast, wherethere are no natural harbours.

Since 1912, in spite of the immense cost and the difficulty of obtaininglabour, the following has been done:

Casablanca. A jetty 1900 metres long has been planned: 824 metresfinished December, 1917.

Small jetty begun 1916, finished 1917: length 330 metres. Small harbourthus created shelters small boats (150 tons) in all weathers.

Quays 747 metres long already finished.

16 steam-cranes working.

Warehouses and depots covering 41,985 square metres completed.

Rabat. Work completed December, 1917.

A quay 200 metres long, to which boats with a draught of three metrescan tie up.

Two groups of warehouses, steam-cranes, etc., covering 22,600 squaremetres.

A quay 100 metres long on the Salé side of the river.

Kenitra. The port of Kenitra is at the mouth of the Sebou River, andis capable of becoming a good river port.

The work up to December, 1917, comprises:

A channel 100 metres long and three metres deep, cut through the bar ofthe Sebou.

Jetties built on each side of the channel.

Quay 100 metres long.

Building of sheds, depots, warehouses, steam-cranes, etc.

At the ports of Fedalah, Mazagan, Safi, Mogador and Agadir similar plansare in course of execution.

COMMERCE
COMPARATIVE TABLES

1912	1918
Total Commerce	Total Commerce
Fcs. 177,737,723	Fcs. 386,238,618
Exports	
Fcs. 67,080,383	Fcs. 116,148,081

ROADS BUILT
National roads   2,074 kilometres
Secondary roads 569 "

RAILWAYS BUILT
622 kilometres

LAND CULTIVATED

1915	1918
Approximate area	Approximate area
21,165.17 hectares	1,681,308.03 hectares

JUSTICE

1. Creation of French courts for French nationals and those under Frenchprotection. These take cognizance of civil cases where both parties, oreven one, are amenable to French jurisdiction.

2. Moroccan law is Moslem, and administered by Moslem magistrates.Private law, including that of inheritance, is based on the Koran. TheSultan has maintained the principle whereby real property andadministrative cases fall under native law. These courts are as far aspossible supervised and controlled by the establishment of a CherifianMinistry of Justice to which the native Judges are responsible. Specialcare is taken to prevent the alienation of property held collectively,or any similar transactions likely to produce political and economicdisturbances.

3. Criminal jurisdiction is delegated to Pashas and Cadis by the Sultan,except of offenses committed against, or in conjunction with, Frenchnationals and those under French protection. Such cases come before thetribunals of the French Protectorate.

EDUCATION

The object of the Protectorate has been, on the one hand, to give to thechildren of French colonists in Morocco the same education as they wouldhave received at elementary and secondary schools in France; on theother, to provide the indigenous population with a system of educationthat shall give to the young Moroccans an adequate commercial or manualtraining, or prepare them for administrative posts, but withoutinterfering with their native customs or beliefs.

Before 1912 there existed in Morocco only a few small schools supportedby the French Legation at Tangier and by the Alliance Française, and agroup of Hebrew schools in the Mellahs, maintained by the UniversalIsraelite Alliance.

1912. Total number of schools 37
1918. " " " " 191

1912. Total number of pupils 3006
1918. " " " " 21,520

1912. Total number of teachers 61
1918.   "   "   "   "   668

In addition to the French and indigenous schools, sewing-schools have been formed for the native girls and have been exceptionally successful.

Moslem colleges have been founded at Rabat and Fez in order to supplement the native education of young Mahometans of the upperclasses, who intend to take up wholesale business or banking, or prepare for political, judicial or administrative posts under the Sultan's government. The course lasts four years and comprises: Arabic, French, mathematics, history, geography, religious (Mahometan) instruction, and the law of the Koran.

The "Ecole Supérieure de la langue arabe et des dialectes berbères" at Rabat receives European and Moroccan students. The courses are: Arabic, the Berber dialects, Arab literature, ethnography, administrative Moroccan law, Moslem law, Berber customary law.

MEDICAL AID

The Protectorate has established 113 medical centres for the native population, ranging from simple dispensaries and small native infirmaries to the important hospitals of Rabat, Fez, Meknez, Marrakech, and Casablanca.

Mobile sanitary formations supplied with light motor ambulances travel about the country, vaccinating, making tours of sanitary inspection, investigating infected areas, and giving general hygienic education throughout the remoter regions.

Native patients treated in 1916   over 900,000
      "   "   "   " 1917   "   1,220,800

Night-shelters in towns. Every town is provided with a shelter for the indigent wayfarers so numerous in Morocco. These shelters are used as disinfection centres, from which suspicious cases are sent to quarantine camp at the gates of the towns.

Central Laboratory at Rabat. This is a kind of Pasteur Institute. In 1917, 210,000 persons were vaccinated throughout the country and 356 patients treated at the Laboratory for rabies.

Clinics for venereal diseases have been established at Casablanca, Fez, Rabat, and Marrakech.

More than 15,000 cases were treated in 1917.

Ophthalmic clinics in the same cities gave in 1917, 44,600consultations.

Radiotherapy. Clinics have been opened at Fez and Rabat for thetreatment of skin diseases of the head, from which the native childrenhabitually suffer.

The French Department of Health distributes annually immense quantitiesof quinine in the malarial districts.

Madame Lyautey's private charities comprise admirably administeredchild-welfare centres in the principal cities, with dispensaries for thenative mothers and children.

VII
A SKETCH OF MOROCCAN HISTORY

NOTE.—In the chapters on Moroccan history and art I have tried to setdown a slight and superficial outline of a large and confused subject.In extenuation of this summary attempt I hasten to explain that itschief merit is its lack of originality.

Its facts are chiefly drawn from the books mentioned in the shortbibliography at the end of the volume; in addition to which I am deeplyindebted for information given on the spot to the group of remarkablespecialists attached to the French administration, and to the cultivatedand cordial French officials, military and civilian, who, at each stageof my rapid journey, did their best to answer my questions and open myeyes.

I

THE BERBERS

In the briefest survey of the Moroccan past account must first of all betaken of the factor which, from the beginning of recorded events, hasconditioned the whole history of North Africa: the existence, from theSahara to the Mediterranean, of a mysterious irreducible indigenous racewith which every successive foreign rule, from Carthage to France, hashad to reckon, and which has but imperfectly and partially assimilatedthe language, the religion, and the culture that successivecivilizations have tried to impose upon it.

This race, the race of Berbers, has never, modern explorers tell us,become really Islamite, any more than it ever really became Phenician,Roman or Vandal. It has imposed its habits while it appeared to adoptthose of its invaders, and has perpetually represented, outside theIsmalitic and Hispano-Arabic circle of the Makhzen, the vast tormentingelement of the dissident, the rebellious, the unsubdued tribes of theBlad-es-Siba.

Who were these indigenous tribes with whom the Phenicians, when theyfounded their first counting-houses on the north and west coast ofAfrica, exchanged stuffs and pottery and arms for ivory,ostrich-feathers and slaves?

Historians frankly say they do not know. All sorts of material obstacleshave hitherto hampered the study of Berber origins; but it seems clearthat from the earliest historic times they were a mixed race, and theethnologist who attempts to define them is faced by the same problem asthe historian of modern America who should try to find the racialdefinition of an "American." For centuries, for ages, North Africa hasbeen what America now is: the clearing-house of the world. When atlength it occurred to the explorer that the natives of North Africa werenot all Arabs or Moors, he was bewildered by the many vistas of all theywere or might be: so many and tangled were the threads leading up tothem, so interwoven was their pre-Islamite culture with worn-out shredsof older and richer societies.

M. Saladin, in his "Manuel d'Architecture Musulmane," after attemptingto unravel the influences which went to the making of the mosque ofKairouan, the walls of Marrakech, the Medersas of Fez—influences thatlead him back to Chaldæan branch-huts, to the walls of Babylon and theembroideries of Coptic Egypt—somewhat despairingly sums up the result:"The principal elements contributed to Moslem art by the stylespreceding it may be thus enumerated: from India, floral ornament; fromPersia, the structural principles of the Acheminedes, and the Sassanianvault. Mesopotamia contributes a system of vaulting, incised ornament,and proportion; the Copts, ornamental detail in general; Egypt, mass andunbroken wall-spaces; Spain, construction and Romano-Iberian ornament;Africa, decorative detail and Romano-Berber traditions (with Byzantineinfluences in Persia); Asia Minor, a mixture of Byzantine and Persiancharacteristics."

As with the art of North Africa, so with its supposedly indigenouspopulation. The Berber dialects extend from the Lybian desert toSenegal. Their language was probably related to Coptic, itself relatedto the ancient Egyptian and the non-Semitic dialects of Abyssinia andNubia. Yet philologists have discovered what appears to be a far-offlink between the Berber and Semitic languages, and the Chleuhs of theDraa and the Souss, with their tall slim Egyptian-looking bodies andhooked noses, may have a strain of Semitic blood. M. Augustin Bernard,in speaking of the natives of

North Africa, ends, much on the same noteas M. Saladin in speaking of Moslem art: "In their blood are thesediments of many races, Phenician, Punic, Egyptian and Arab."

They were not, like the Arabs, wholly nomadic; but the tent, the flock,the tribe always entered into their conception of life. M. AugustinBernard has pointed out that, in North Africa, the sedentary and nomadichabit do not imply a permanent difference, but rather a temporary one ofsituation and opportunity. The sedentary Berbers are nomadic in certainconditions; and from the earliest times the invading nomad Berberstended to become sedentary when they reached the rich plains north ofthe Atlas. But when they built cities it was as their ancestors andtheir neighbours pitched tents; and they destroyed or abandoned them aslightly as their desert forbears packed their camel-bags and moved tonew pastures. Everywhere behind the bristling walls and rock-clampedtowers of old Morocco lurks the shadowy spirit of instability. Every newSultan builds himself a new house and lets his predecessors' palacesfall into decay; and as with the Sultan so with his vassals andofficials. Change is the rule in this apparently unchanged civilization,where "nought may abide but Mutability."

II
PHENICIANS, ROMANS AND VANDALS
Far to the south of the Anti-Atlas, in the yellow deserts that lead toTimbuctoo, live the wild Touaregs, the Veiled Men of the south, who rideto war with their faces covered by linen masks.

These Veiled Men are Berbers; but their alphabet is composed of Lybiancharacters, and these are closely related to the signs engraved oncertain vases of the Nile valley that are probably six thousand yearsold. Moreover, among the rock-cut images of the African desert is thelikeness of Theban Ammon crowned with the solar disk between serpents;and the old Berber religion, with its sun and animal worship, has manypoints of resemblance with Egyptian beliefs. All this implies tradecontacts far below the horizon of history, and obscure comings andgoings of restless throngs across incredible distances long before thePhenicians planted their first trading posts on the north African coastabout 1200 B. C.

Five hundred years before Christ, Carthage sent one of her admirals on avoyage of colonization beyond the Pillars of Hercules. Hannon set outwith sixty fifty-oared galleys carrying thirty thousand people. Some ofthem settled at Mehedyia, at the mouth of the Sebou, where Phenicianremains have been found; and apparently the exploration was pushed asfar south as the coast of Guinea, for the inscription recording itrelates that Hannon beheld elephants, hairy men and "savages calledgorillas." At any rate, Carthage founded stable colonies at Melilla,Larache, Salé and Casablanca.

Then came the Romans, who carried on the business, set up one of theireasy tolerant protectorates over "Tingitanian Mauretania," and builtone important military outpost, Volubilis in the Zerhoun, which a seriesof minor defenses probably connected with Salé on the west coast, thusguarding the Roman province against the unconquered Berbers to thesouth.

Tingitanian Mauretania was one of the numerous African granaries ofRome. She also supplied the Imperial armies with their famous Africancavalry; and among minor articles of exportation were guinea-hens,snails, honey, euphorbia, wild beasts, horses and pearls. The Romandominion ceased at the line drawn between Volubilis and Salé. There wasno interest in pushing farther south, since the ivory and slave tradewith the Soudan was carried on by way of Tripoli. But the spirit ofenterprise never slept in the race, and Pliny records the journey of aRoman general—Suetonius Paulinus—who appears to have crossed theAtlas, probably by the pass of Tizi-n-Telremt, which is even now sobeset with difficulties that access by land to the Souss will remain anarduous undertaking until the way by Imintanout is safe for Europeantravel.

The Vandals swept away the Romans in the fifth century. The Lower Empirerestored a brief period of civilization; but its authority finallydwindled to the half-legendary rule of Count Julian, shut up within hiswalls of Ceuta. Then Europe vanished from the shores of Africa; andthough Christianity lingered here and there in vague Donatist colonies,and in the names of Roman bishoprics, its last faint hold went down inthe eighth century before the irresistible cry: "There is no God butAllah!"

III

THE ARAB CONQUEST

The first Arab invasion of Morocco is said to have reached the Atlanticcoast; but it left no lasting traces, and the real Islamisation ofBarbary did not happen till near the end of the eighth century, when adescendant of Ali, driven from Mesopotamia by the Caliphate, reached themountains above Volubilis and there founded an empire. The Berbers,though indifferent in religious matters, had always, from a spirit ofindependence, tended to heresy and schism. Under the rule of ChristianRome they had been Donatists, as M. Bernard puts it, "out of oppositionto the Empire"; and so, out of opposition to the Caliphate, they took upthe cause of one Moslem schismatic after another. Their great popularmovements have always had a religious basis, or perhaps it would betruer to say, a religious pretext; for they have been in reality thepartly moral, partly envious revolt of hungry and ascetic warrior tribesagainst the fatness and corruption of the "cities of the plain."

Idriss I became the first national saint and ruler of Morocco. His ruleextended throughout northern Morocco, and his son, Idriss II, attackinga Berber tribe on the banks of the Oued Fez, routed them, tookpossession of their oasis and founded the city of Fez. Thither cameschismatic refugees from Kairouan and Moors from Andalusia. The IslamiteEmpire of Morocco was founded, and Idriss II has become the legendaryancestor of all its subsequent rulers.

The Idrissite rule is a welter of obscure struggles between rapidlymelting groups of adherents. Its chief features are: the founding ofMoulay Idriss and Fez, and the building of the mosques of El Andalousand Kairouiyin at Fez for the two groups of refugees from Tunisia andSpain. Meanwhile the Caliphate of Cordova had reached the height of itspower, while that of the Fatimites extended from the Nile to westernMorocco, and the little Idrissite empire, pulverized under the weight ofthese expanding powers, became once more a dust of disintegrated tribes.

It was only in the eleventh century that the dust again conglomerated.Two Arab tribes from the desert of the Hedjaz, suddenly driven westwardby the Fatimites, entered Morocco, not with a small military expedition,as the Arabs had hitherto done, but with a horde of emigrants reckonedas high as 200,000 families; and this first colonizing expedition wasdoubtless succeeded by others.

To strengthen their hold in Morocco the Arab colonists embraced thedynastic feuds of the Berbers. They inaugurated a period of generalhavoc which destroyed what little prosperity had survived the break-upof the Idrissite rule, and many Berber tribes took refuge in themountains; but others remained and were merged with the invaders,reforming into new tribes of mixed Berber and Arab blood. This invasionwas almost purely destructive; it marks one of the most desolate periodsin the progress of the "wasteful Empire" of Moghreb.

IV
ALMORAVIDS AND ALMOHADS

While the Hilalian Arabs were conquering and destroying northern Moroccoanother but more fruitful invasion was upon her from the south. TheAlmoravids, one of the tribes of Veiled Men of the south, driven by theusual mixture of religious zeal and lust of booty, set out to invade therich black kingdoms north of the Sahara. Thence they crossed the Atlasunder their great chief, Youssef-ben-Tachfin, and founded the city ofMarrakech in 1062. From Marrakech they advanced on Idrissite Fez and thevalley of the Moulouya. Fez rose against her conquerors, and Youssefput all the male inhabitants to death. By 1084 he was master of Tangierand the Rif, and his rule stretched as far west as Tlemcen, Oran andfinally Algiers.

His ambition drove him across the straits to Spain, where he conqueredone Moslem prince after another and wiped out the luxurious civilizationof Moorish Andalusia. In 1086, at Zallarca, Youssef gave battle toAlphonso VI of Castile and Leon. The Almoravid army was a strange rabbleof Arabs, Berbers, blacks, wild tribes of the Sahara and Christianmercenaries. They conquered the Spanish forces, and Youssef left to hissuccessors an empire extending from the Ebro to Senegal and from theAtlantic coast of Africa to the borders of Tunisia. But the empire fellto pieces of its own weight, leaving little record of its brief andstormy existence. While Youssef was routing the forces of Christianityat Zallarca in Spain, another schismatic tribe of his own people wasdetaching Marrakech and the south from his rule.

The leader of the new invasion was a Mahdi, one of the numerous Savioursof the World who have carried death and destruction throughout Islam.His name was Ibn-Toumert, and he had travelled in Egypt, Syria andSpain, and made the pilgrimage to Mecca. Preaching the doctrine of apurified monotheism, he called his followers the Almohads or Unitarians,to distinguish them from the polytheistic Almoravids, whose heresies hedenounced. He fortified the city of Tinmel in the Souss, and built therea mosque of which the ruins still exist. When he died, in 1128, hedesignated as his successor Abd-el-Moumen, the son of a potter, who hadbeen his disciple.

Abd-el-Moumen carried on the campaign against the Almoravids. He foughtthem not only in Morocco but in Spain, taking Cadiz, Cordova, Granada aswell as Tlemcen and Fez. In 1152 his African dominion reached fromTripoli to the Souss, and he had formed a disciplined army in whichChristian mercenaries from France and Spain fought side by side withBerbers and Soudanese. This great captain was also a greatadministrator, and under his rule Africa was surveyed from the Souss toBarka, the country was policed, agriculture was protected, and thecaravans journeyed safely over the trade-routes.

Abd-el-Moumen died in 1163 and was followed by his son, who, though hesuffered reverses in Spain, was also a great ruler. He died in 1184, andhis son, Yacoub-el-Mansour, avenged his father's ill-success in Spain bythe great victory of Alarcos and the conquest of Madrid.Yacoub-el-Mansour was the greatest of Moroccan Sultans. So far did hisfame extend that the illustrious Saladin sent him presents and asked thehelp of his fleet. He was a builder as well as a fighter, and thenoblest period of Arab art in Morocco and Spain coincides with hisreign.

After his death, the Almohad empire followed the downward curve to whichall Oriental rule seems destined. In Spain, the Berber forces werebeaten in the great Christian victory of Las-Navas-de Tolosa; and inMorocco itself the first stirrings of the Beni-Merins (a new tribe fromthe Sahara) were preparing the way for a new dynasty.

V

THE MERINIDS

The Beni-Merins or Merinids were nomads who ranged the desert betweenBiskra and the Tafilelt. It was not a religious upheaval that drove themto the conquest of Morocco. The demoralized Almohads called them in asmercenaries to defend their crumbling empire; and the Merinids came,drove out the Almohads, and replaced them.

They took Fez, Meknez, Salé, Rabat and Sidjilmassa in the Tafilelt; andtheir second Sultan, Abou-Youssef, built New Fez (Eldjid) on the heightabove the old Idrissite city. The Merinids renewed the struggle with theSultan of Tlemcen, and carried the Holy War once more into Spain. Theconflict with Tlemcen was long and unsuccessful, and one of the MerinidSultans died assassinated under its walls. In the fourteenth century theSultan Abou Hassan tried to piece together the scattered bits of theAlmohad empire. Tlemcen was finally taken, and the whole of Algeriaannexed. But in the plain of Kairouan, in Tunisia, Abou Hassan wasdefeated by the Arabs. Meanwhile one of his brothers had headed a revoltin Morocco, and the princes of Tlemcen won back their ancient kingdom.Constantine and Bougie rebelled in turn, and the kingdom of Abou Hassanvanished like a mirage. His successors struggled vainly to controltheir vassals in Morocco, and to keep their possessions beyond itsborders. Before the end of the fourteenth century Morocco from end toend was a chaos of antagonistic tribes, owning no allegiance, abiding byno laws. The last of the Merinids, divided, diminished, bound byhumiliating treaties with Christian Spain, kept up a semblance ofsovereignty at Fez and Marrakech, at war with one another and with theirneighbours; and Spain and Portugal seized this moment of internaldissolution to drive them from Spain, and carry the war into Moroccoitself.

The short and stormy passage of the Beni-Merins seems hardly to leaveroom for the development of the humaner qualities; yet the flowering ofMoroccan art and culture coincided with those tumultuous years, and itwas under the Merinid Sultans that Fez became the centre of Moroccanlearning and industry, a kind of Oxford with Birmingham annexed.

VI

THE SAADIANS

Meanwhile, behind all the Berber turmoil a secret work of religiouspropaganda was going on. The Arab element had been crushed but notextirpated. The crude idolatrous wealth-loving Berbers apparentlydominated; but whenever there was a new uprising or a new invasion itwas based on the religious discontent perpetually stirred up byMahometan agents. The longing for a Mahdi, a Saviour, the craving forpurification combined with an opportunity to murder and rob, always gavethe Moslem apostle a ready opening; and the downfall of the Merinids wasthe result of a long series of religious movements to which the Europeaninvasion gave an object and a war-cry.

The Saadians were Cherifian Arabs, newcomers from Arabia, to whom thelax Berber paganism was abhorrent. They preached a return to the creedof Mahomet, and proclaimed the Holy War against the hated Portuguese,who had set up fortified posts all along the west coast of Morocco.

It is a mistake to suppose that hatred of the Christian has alwaysexisted among the North African Moslems. The earlier dynasties, andespecially the great Almohad Sultans, were on friendly terms with theCatholic powers of Europe, and in the thirteenth century a treatyassured to Christians in Africa full religious liberty, excepting onlythe right to preach their doctrine in public places. There was aCatholic diocese at Fez, and afterward at Marrakech under Gregory IX,and there is a letter of the Pope thanking the "Miromilan" (the Emir ElMoumenin) for his kindness to the Bishop and the friars living in hisdominions. Another Bishop was recommended by Innocent IV to the Sultanof Morocco; the Pope even asked that certain strongholds should beassigned to the Christians in Morocco as places of refuge in times ofdisturbance. But the best proof of the friendly relations betweenChristians and infidels is the fact that the Christian armies whichhelped the Sultans of Morocco to defeat Spain and subjugate Algeria andTunisia were not composed of "renegadoes" or captives, as is generallysupposed, but of Christian mercenaries, French and English, led byknights and nobles, and fighting for the Sultan of Morocco exactly asthey would have fought for the Duke of Burgundy, the Count of Flanders,or any other Prince who offered high pay and held out the hope of richspoils. Any one who has read

"Villehardouin" and "Joinville" will ownthat there is not much to choose between the motives animating thesenoble freebooters and those which caused the Crusaders to lootConstantinople "on the way" to the Holy Sepulchre. War in those days wasregarded as a lucrative and legitimate form of business, exactly as itwas when the earlier heroes started out to take the rich robber-town ofTroy.

The Berbers have never been religious fanatics, and the Vicomte deFoucauld, when he made his great journey of exploration in the Atlas in1883, remarked that antagonism to the foreigner was always due to thefear of military espionage and never to religious motives. This equallyapplies to the Berbers of the sixteenth century, when the Holy Waragainst Catholic Spain and Portugal was preached. The real cause of thesudden deadly hatred of the foreigner was twofold. The Spaniards weredetested because of the ferocious cruelty with which they had driven theMoors from Spain under Ferdinand and Isabella; and the Portuguesebecause of the arrogance and brutality of their military colonists inthe fortified trading stations of the west coast. And both were fearedas possible conquerors and overlords.

There was a third incentive also: the Moroccans, dealing in black slavesfor the European market, had discovered the value of white slaves inMoslem markets. The Sultan had his fleet, and each coast-town itspowerful pirate vessels, and from pirate-nests like Salé and Tangier theraiders continued, till well on into the first half of the nineteenthcentury, to seize European ships and carry their passengers to theslave-markets of Fez and Marrakech. The miseries endured by thesecaptives, and so poignantly described in John Windus's travels, and inthe "Naufrage du Brick Sophie" by Charles Cochelet, show how savagethe feeling against the foreigner had become.

With the advent of the Cherifian dynasties, which coincided with thisreligious reform, and was in fact brought about by it, Morocco became aclosed country, as fiercely guarded as Japan against Europeanpenetration. Cut off from civilizing influences, the Moslems isolatedthemselves in a lonely fanaticism, far more racial than religious, andthe history of the country from the fall of the Merinids till the Frenchannexation is mainly a dull tale of tribal warfare.

The religious movement of the sixteenth century was led and fed byzealots from the Sahara. One of them took possession of Rabat andAzemmour, and preached the Holy War; other "feudal fiefs" (as M.Augustin Bernard has well called them) were founded at Tameslout, Ilegh,Tamgrout: the tombs of the *marabouts* who led these revolts arescattered all along the west coast, and are still objects of popularveneration. The unorthodox saint worship which marks Moroccan Moslemism,and is commemorated by the countless white *koubbas* throughout thecountry, grew up chiefly at the time of the religious revival under theSaadian dynasty, and almost all the "Moulays" and "Sidis" veneratedbetween Tangier and the Atlas were warrior monks who issued forth fromtheir fortified *Zaouïas* to drive the Christians out of Africa.

The Saadians were probably rather embarrassed by these fanatics, whomthey found useful to oppose to the Merinids, but troublesome where theirown plans were concerned. They were ambitious and luxury-loving princes,who invaded the wealthy kingdom of the Soudan, conquered the Sultan ofTimbuctoo, and came back laden with slaves and gold to embellishMarrakech and spend their treasure in the usual demoralizing orgies.Their exquisite tombs at Marrakech commemorate in courtly language thesuperhuman virtues of a series of rulers whose debaucheries and viceswere usually cut short by assassination. Finally another austere andfanatical mountain tribe surged down on them, wiped them out, and ruledin their stead.

VII
THE HASSANIANS

The new rulers came from the Tafilelt, which has always been atroublesome corner of Morocco. The first two Hassanian Sultans were theusual tribal chiefs bent on taking advantage of Saadian misrule to lootand conquer. But the third was the great Moulay-Ismaël, the tale ofwhose long and triumphant rule (1672 to 1727) has already been told inthe chapter on Meknez. This savage and enlightened old man once moredrew order out of anarchy, and left, when he died, an organized andadministered empire, as well as a progeny of seven hundred sons andunnumbered daughters.

The empire fell apart as usual, and no less quickly than usual, underhis successors; and from his death until the strong hand of GeneralLyautey took over the direction of affairs the Hassanian rule in Moroccowas little more than a tumult of incoherent ambitions. The successors ofMoulay-Ismaël inherited his blood-lust and his passion for dominionwithout his capacity to govern. In 1757 Sidi-Mohammed, one of his sons,tried to put order into his kingdom, and drove the last Portuguese outof Morocco; but under his successors the country remained isolated andstagnant, making spasmodic efforts to defend itself against theencroachments of European influence, while its rulers wasted theirenergy in a policy of double-dealing and dissimulation. Early in thenineteenth century the government was compelled by the European powersto suppress piracy and the trade in Christian slaves; and in 1830 theFrench conquest of Algeria broke down the wall of isolation behind whichthe country was mouldering away by placing a European power on one ofits frontiers.

At first the conquest of Algeria tended to create a link between Franceand Morocco. The Dey of Algiers was a Turk, and, therefore, anhereditary enemy; and Morocco was disposed to favour the power which hadbroken Turkish rule in a neighbouring country. But the Sultan could nothelp trying to profit by the general disturbance to seize Tlemcen andraise insurrections in western Algeria; and presently Morocco wasengaged in a Holy War against France. Abd-el-Kader, the Sultan ofAlgeria, had taken refuge in Morocco, and the Sultan of Morocco havingfurnished him with supplies and munitions, France sent an officialremonstrance. At the same time Marshal Bugeaud landed at Mers-el-Kebir,and invited the Makhzen to discuss the situation. The offer was acceptedand General Bedeau and the Caïd El Guennaoui met in an open place.Behind them their respective troops were drawn up, and almost as soonas the first salutes were exchanged the Caïd declared the negotiationsbroken off. The French troops accordingly withdrew to the coast, butduring their retreat they were attacked by the Moroccans. This put anend to peaceful negotiations, and Tangier was besieged and taken. Thefollowing August Bugeaud brought his troops up from Oudjda, through thedefile that leads from West Algeria, and routed the Moroccans. He wishedto advance on Fez, but international politics interfered, and he was notallowed to carry out his plans. England looked unfavourably on theFrench penetration of Morocco, and it became necessary to conclude peaceat once to prove that France had no territorial ambitions west ofOudjda.

Meanwhile a great Sultan was once more to appear in the land.Moulay-el-Hassan, who ruled from 1873 to 1894, was an able and energeticadministrator. He pieced together his broken empire, asserted hisauthority in Fez and Marrakech, and fought the rebellious tribes of thewest. In 1877 he asked the French government to send him a permanentmilitary mission to assist in organizing his army. He planned anexpedition to the Souss, but the want of food and water in thewilderness traversed by the army caused the most cruel sufferings.Moulay-el-Hassan had provisions sent by sea, but the weather was toostormy to allow of a landing on the exposed Atlantic coast, and theSultan, who had never seen the sea, was as surprised and indignant asCanute to find that the waves would not obey him.

His son Abd-el-Aziz was only thirteen years old when he succeeded to thethrone. For six years he remained under the guardianship of Ba-Ahmed,the black Vizier of Moulay-el-Hassan, who built the fairy palace of theBahia at Marrakech, with its mysterious pale green padlocked doorleading down to the secret vaults where his treasure was hidden. Whenthe all-powerful Ba-Ahmed died the young Sultan was nineteen. He wasintelligent, charming, and fond of the society of Europeans; but he wasindifferent to religious questions and still more to military affairs,and thus doubly at the mercy of native mistrust and European intrigue.

Some clumsy attempts at fiscal reform, and a too great leaning towardEuropean habits and associates, roused the animosity of the people, andof the conservative party in the upper class. The Sultan's eldestbrother, who had been set aside in his favour, was intriguing againsthim; the usual Cherifian Pretender was stirring up the factious tribesin the mountains; and the European powers were attempting, in theconfusion of an ungoverned country, to assert their respectiveascendencies.

The demoralized condition of the country justified these attempts, andmade European interference inevitable. But the powers were jealouslywatching each other, and Germany, already coveting the certainagricultural resources and the conjectured mineral wealth of Morocco,was above all determined that a French protectorate should not be setup.

In 1908 another son of Moulay-Hassan, Abd-el-Hafid, was proclaimedSultan by the reactionary Islamite faction, who accused Abd-el-Aziz ofhaving sold his country to the Christians. Abd-el-Aziz was defeated in abattle near Marrakech, and retired to Tangier, where he still lives infutile state. Abd-el-Hafid, proclaimed Sultan at Fez, was recognized bythe whole country; but he found himself unable to cope with the factioustribes (those outside the Blad-el-Makhzen, or *governed country*). Theserebel tribes besieged Fez, and the Sultan had to ask France for aid.France sent troops to his relief, but as soon as the dissidents wererouted, and he himself was safe, Abd-el-Hafid refused to give the Frencharmy his support, and in 1912, after the horrible massacres of Fez, heabdicated in favour of another brother, Moulay Youssef, the actual rulerof Morocco.

VIII
NOTE ON MOROCCAN
ARCHITECTURE

I

M. H. Saladin, whose "Manual of Moslem Architecture" was published in1907, ends his chapter on Morocco with the words: "It is especiallyurgent that we should know, and penetrate into, Morocco as soon aspossible, in order to study its monuments. It is the only country butPersia where Moslem art actually survives; and the tradition handed downto the present day will doubtless clear up many things."

M. Saladin's wish has been partly realized. Much has been done since1912, when General Lyautey was appointed Resident-General, to clear upand classify the history of Moroccan art; but since 1914, though thework has never been dropped, it has necessarily been much delayed,especially as regards its published record; and as yet only a fewmonographs and articles have summed up some of the interestinginvestigations of the last five years.

II

When I was in Marrakech word was sent to Captain de S., who was with me,that a Caïd of the Atlas, whose prisoner he had been several yearsbefore, had himself been taken by the Pasha's troops, and was inMarrakech. Captain de S. was asked to identify several rifles which hisold enemy had taken from him, and on receiving them found that, in theinterval, they had been elaborately ornamented with the Arab niello workof which the tradition goes back to Damascus.

This little incident is a good example of the degree to which themediæval tradition alluded to by M. Saladin has survived in Moroccanlife. Nowhere else in the world, except among the moribundfresco-painters of the Greek monasteries, has a formula of art persistedfrom the seventh or eighth century to the present day; and in Moroccothe formula is not the mechanical expression of a petrified theology butthe setting of the life of a people who have gone on wearing the same clothes, observing the same customs, believing in the same fetiches, and using the same saddles, ploughs, looms, and dye-stuffs as in the days when the foundations of the first mosque of El Kairouiyin were laid.

The origin of this tradition is confused and obscure. The Arabs have never been creative artists, nor are the Berbers known to have been so. As investigations proceed in Syria and Mesopotamia it seems more and more probable that the sources of inspiration of pre-Moslem art in North Africa are to be found in Egypt, Persia, and India. Each new investigation pushes these sources farther back and farther east; but it is not of much use to retrace these ancient vestiges, since Moroccan art has, so far, nothing to show of pre-Islamite art, save what is purely Phenician or Roman.

In any case, however, it is not in Morocco that the clue to Moroccan art is to be sought; though interesting hints and mysterious reminiscences will doubtless be found in such places as Tinmel, in the gorges of the Atlas, where a ruined mosque of the earliest Almohad period has been photographed by M. Doutté, and in the curious Algerian towns of Sedrata and the Kalaa of the Beni Hammads. Both of these latter towns were rich and prosperous communities in the tenth century and both were destroyed in the eleventh, so that they survive as mediæval Pompeiis of a quite exceptional interest, since their architecture appears to have been almost unaffected by classic or Byzantine influences.

Traces of a very old indigenous art are found in the designs on the modern white and black Berber pottery; but this work, specimens of which are to be seen in the Oriental Department of the Louvre, seems to go back, by way of Central America, Greece (sixth century B. C.) and Susa (twelfth century B. C.), to the far-off period before the streams of human invention had divided, and when the same loops and ripples and spirals formed on the flowing surface of every current.

It is a disputed question whether Spanish influence was foremost in developing the peculiarly Moroccan art of the earliest Moslem period, or whether European influences came by way of Syria and Palestine, and afterward met and were crossed with those of Moorish Spain. Probably both things happened, since the Almoravids were in Spain; and no doubt the currents met and mingled. At any rate, Byzantine, Greece, and thePalestine and Syria of the Crusaders, contributed as much as Rome andGreece to the formation of that peculiar Moslem art which, all the wayfrom India to the Pillars of Hercules, built itself, with minorvariations, out of the same elements.

Arab conquerors always destroy as much as they can of the work of theirpredecessors, and nothing remains, as far as is known, of Almoravidarchitecture in Morocco. But the great Almohad Sultans covered Spain andNorthwest Africa with their monuments, and no later buildings in Africaequal them in strength and majesty.

It is no doubt because the Almohads built in stone that so much of whatthey made survives. The Merinids took to rubble and a soft tufa, and theCherifian dynasties built in clay like the Spaniards in South America.And so seventeenth century Meknez has perished while the Almohad wallsand towers of the tenth century still stand.

The principal old buildings of Morocco are defensive and religious—andunder the latter term the beautiful collegiate houses (the medersas) ofFez and Salé may fairly be included, since the educational system ofIslam is essentially and fundamentally theological. Of old secularbuildings, palaces or private houses, virtually none are known toexist; but their plan and decorations may easily be reconstituted fromthe early chronicles, and also from the surviving palaces built in theeighteenth and nineteenth centuries, and even those which the wealthynobles of modern Morocco are building to this day.

The whole of civilian Moslem architecture from Persia to Morocco isbased on four unchanging conditions: a hot climate, slavery, polygamyand the segregation of women. The private house in Mahometan countriesis in fact a fortress, a convent and a temple: a temple of which the god(as in all ancient religions) frequently descends to visit hiscloistered votaresses. For where slavery and polygamy exist everyhouse-master is necessarily a god, and the house he inhabits a shrinebuilt about his divinity.

The first thought of the Moroccan chieftain was always defensive. Assoon as he pitched a camp or founded a city it had to be guarded againstthe hungry hordes who encompassed him on every side. Each little centreof culture and luxury in Moghreb was an islet in a sea of perpetualstorms. The wonder is that, thus incessantly threatened from without andconspired against from within—with the desert at their doors, andtheir slaves on the threshold—these violent men managed to create aboutthem an atmosphere of luxury and stability that astonished not only theobsequious native chronicler but travellers and captives from westernEurope.

The truth is, as has been often pointed out, that, even until the end ofthe seventeenth century, the refinements of civilization were in manyrespects no greater in France and England than in North Africa. NorthAfrica had long been in more direct communication with the old Empiresof immemorial luxury, and was therefore farther advanced in the arts ofliving than the Spain and France of the Dark Ages; and this is why, in acountry that to the average modern European seems as savage as Ashantee,one finds traces of a refinement of life and taste hardly to be matchedby Carlovingian and early Capetian Europe.

III

The brief Almoravid dynasty left no monuments behind it.

Fez had already been founded by the Idrissites, and its first mosques(Kairouiyin and Les Andalous) existed. Of the Almoravid Fez andMarrakech the chroniclers relate great things; but the wild Hilalianinvasion and the subsequent descent of the Almohads from the High Atlasswept away whatever the first dynasties had created.

The Almohads were mighty builders, and their great monuments are all ofstone. The earliest known example of their architecture which hassurvived is the ruined mosque of Tinmel, in the High Atlas, discoveredand photographed by M. Doutté. This mosque was built by the inspiredmystic, Ibn-Toumert, who founded the line. Following him came the greatpalace-making Sultans whose walled cities of splendid mosques and towershave Romanesque qualities of mass and proportion, and, as M. RaymondKoechlin has pointed out, inevitably recall the "robust simplicity ofthe master builders who at the very same moment were beginning in Francethe construction of the first Gothic cathedrals and the noblest feudalcastles."

In the thirteenth century, with the coming of the Merinids, Moroccanarchitecture grew more delicate, more luxurious, and perhaps also morepeculiarly itself. That interaction of Spanish and Arab art whichproduced the style known as Moorish reached, on the African side of theStraits, its greatest completeness in Morocco. It was under the Merinidsthat Moorish art grew into full beauty in Spain, and under the Merinidsthat Fez rebuilt the mosque Kairouiyin and that of the Andalusians, andcreated six of its nine *Medersas*, the most perfect surviving buildingsof that unique moment of sober elegance and dignity.

The Cherifian dynasties brought with them a decline in taste. A crudedesire for immediate effect, and the tendency toward a more barbaricluxury, resulted in the piling up of frail palaces as impermanent astents. Yet a last flower grew from the deformed and dying trunk of theold Empire. The Saadian Sultan who invaded the Soudan and came backladen with gold and treasure from the great black city of Timbuctoocovered Marrakech with hasty monuments of which hardly a trace survives.But there, in a nettle-grown corner of a ruinous quarter, lay hiddentill yesterday the Chapel of the Tombs: the last emanation of purebeauty of a mysterious, incomplete, forever retrogressive and yetforever forward-straining people. The Merinid tombs of Fez have fallen;but those of their destroyers linger on in precarious grace, like aflower on the edge of a precipice.

IV

Moroccan architecture, then, is easily divided into four groups: thefortress, the mosque, the collegiate building and the private house.

The kernel of the mosque is always the *mihrab*, or niche facing towardthe Kasbah of Mecca, where the *imam* stands to say the prayer. Thisarrangement, which enabled as many as possible of the faithful to kneelfacing the *mihrab*, results in a ground-plan necessarily consisting oflong aisles parallel with the wall of the *mihrab*, to which more andmore aisles are added as the number of worshippers grows. Where therewas not space to increase these lateral aisles they were lengthened ateach end. This typical plan is modified in the Moroccan mosques by awider transverse space, corresponding with the nave of a Christianchurch, and extending across the mosque from the praying niche to theprincipal door. To the right of the *mihrab* is the *minbar*, the carvedpulpit (usually of cedar-wood incrusted with mother-of-pearl and ebony)from which the Koran is read. In some Algerian and Egyptian mosques (andat Cordova, for instance) the *mihrab* is enclosed in a sort of screencalled the *maksoura*; but in Morocco this modification of the simplerplan was apparently not adopted.

The interior construction of the mosque was no doubt usually affected bythe nearness of Roman or Byzantine ruins. M. Saladin points out thatthere seem to be few instances of the use of columns made by nativebuilders; but it does not therefore follow that all the columns used inthe early mosques were taken from Roman temples or Christian basilicas.The Arab invaders brought their architects and engineers with them; andit is very possible that some of the earlier mosques were built byprisoners or fortune-hunters from Greece or Italy or Spain.

At any rate, the column on which the arcades of the vaulting rests inthe earlier mosques, as at Tunis and Kairouan, and the mosque ElKairouiyin at Fez, gives way later to the use of piers, foursquare, orwith flanking engaged pilasters as at Algiers and Tlemcen. The exteriorof the mosques, as a rule, is almost entirely hidden by a mushroomgrowth of buildings, lanes and covered bazaars; but where the outerwalls have remained disengaged they show, as at Kairouan and Cordova,great masses of windowless masonry pierced at intervals with majesticgateways.

Beyond the mosque, and opening into it by many wide doors of beatenbronze or carved cedar-wood, lies the Court of the Ablutions. Theopenings in the façade were multiplied in order that, on great days, thefaithful who were not able to enter the mosque might hear the prayersand catch a glimpse of the *mihrab*.

In a corner of the courts stands the minaret. It is the structure onwhich Moslem art has played the greatest number of variations, cuttingoff its angles, building it on a circular or polygonal plan, andendlessly modifying the pyramids and pendentives by which theground-plan of one story passes into that of the next. These problems oftransition, always fascinating to the architect, led in Persia,Mesopotamia and Egypt to many different compositions and ways oftreatment; but in Morocco the minaret, till modern times, remainedsteadfastly square, and proved that no other plan is so beautiful asthis simplest one of all.

Surrounding the Court of the Ablutions are the school-rooms, librariesand other dependencies, which grew as the Mahometan religion prosperedand Arab culture developed.

The medersa was a farther extension of the mosque: it was the academywhere the Moslem schoolman prepared his theology and the other branchesof strange learning which, to the present day, make up the curriculum ofthe Mahometan university. The medersa is an adaptation of the privatehouse to religious and educational ends; or, if one prefers anotheranalogy, it is a *fondak* built above a miniature mosque. Theground-plan is always the same: in the centre an arcaded court with afountain, on one side the long narrow praying-chapel with the *mihrab*,on the other a class-room with the same ground-plan; and on the nextstory a series of cell-like rooms for the students, opening on carvedcedar-wood balconies. This cloistered plan, where all the effect isreserved for the interior façades about the court, lends itself to adelicacy of detail that would be inappropriate on a street-front; andthe medersas of Fez are endlessly varied in their fanciful but neverexuberant decoration.

M. Tranchant de Lunel has pointed out (in "France-Maroc") with what asure sense of suitability the Merinid architects adapted this decorationto the uses of the buildings. On the lower floor, under the cloister, isa revêtement of marble (often alabaster) or of the almost indestructibleceramic mosaic. On the floor above, massive cedar-wood corbelsending in monsters of almost Gothic inspiration support the frettedbalconies; and above rise stucco interlacings, placed too high up to beinjured by man, and guarded from the weather by projecting eaves.

The private house, whether merchant's dwelling or chieftain's palace, islaid out on the same lines, with the addition of the reserved quartersfor women; and what remains in Spain and Sicily of Moorish seculararchitecture shows that, in the Merinid period, the play of ornamentmust have been—as was natural—even greater than in the medersas.

The Arab chroniclers paint pictures of Merinid palaces, such as theHouse of the Favourite at Cordova, which the soberer modern imaginationrefused to accept until the medersas of Fez were revealed, and the olddecorative tradition was shown in the eighteenth century Moroccanpalaces. The descriptions given of the palaces of Fez and of Marrakechin the preceding articles, which make it unnecessary, in so slight anote as this, to go again into the detail of their planning anddecoration, will serve to show how gracefully the art of the mosque andthe medersa was lightened and domesticated to suit these cool chambersand flower-filled courts.

With regard to the immense fortifications that are the most picturesqueand noticeable architectural features of Morocco, the first thing tostrike the traveller is the difficulty of discerning any difference inthe probable date of their construction until certain structuralpeculiarities are examined, or the ornamental details of the greatgateways are noted. Thus the Almohad portions of the walls of Fez andRabat are built of stone, while later parts are of rubble; and the touchof European influence in certain gateways of Meknez and Fez at oncesituate them in the seventeenth century. But the mediæval outline ofthese great piles of masonry, and certain technicalities in their plan,such as the disposition of the towers, alternating in the inner andouter walls, continued unchanged throughout the different dynasties; andthis immutability of the Moroccan military architecture enables theimagination to picture, not only what was the aspect of the fortifiedcities which the Greeks built in Palestine and Syria, and the Crusadersbrought back to Europe, but even that of the far-off Assyrio-Chaldæanstrongholds to which the whole fortified architecture of the Middle Agesin Europe seems to lead back.

IX
BOOKS CONSULTED

Afrique Française (L'), Bulletin Mensuel du Comité de l'Afrique Française. Paris, 21, rue Cassette.

Bernard, Augustin. Le Maroc. Paris, F. Alcan, 1916.

Budgett-Meakin. The Land of the Moors. London, 1902.

Châtelain, L. Recherches archéologiques au Maroc. Volubilis. (Published by the Military Command in Morocco.)

Les Fouilles de Volubilis. (Extrait du Bulletin Archéologique, 1916.)

Chevrillon, A. Crépuscule d'Islam.

Cochelet, Charles. Le Naufrage du Brick Sophie.

Conférences Marocaines. Paris, Plon-Nourrit.

Doutté, E. En Tribu. Paris, 1914.

Foucauld, Vicomte de. La Reconnaissance au Maroc. Paris, 1888.

France-Maroc. Revue Mensuelle, Paris, 4, rue Chauveau-Lagarde.

Gaillard. Une Ville d'Islam, Fez. Paris, 1909.

Gayet, Al. L'Art Arabe. Paris, 1906.

Houdas, O. Le Maroc de 1631 à 1812. Extrait d'une histoire du Maroc intitulée "L'Interprète qui s'exprime clairement sur les dynasties de l'Orient et de l'Occident" par Ezziani. Paris, E. Leroux, 1886.

Koechlin, Raymond. Une Exposition d'Art Marocain. (Gazette des Beaux-Arts, Juillet-Septembre, 1917.)

Leo Africanus, Description of Africa.

Loti, Pierre. Au Maroc.

Migeon, Gaston. Manuel d'Art Musulman. II. Les Arts Plastiques et Industriels. Paris, A. Picard et Fils, 1907.

Saladin, H. Manuel d'Art Musulman. I. L'Architecture. Paris, A. Picard et Fils, 1907.

Segonzac, Marquis de. Voyages au Maroc. Paris, 1903. Au Cœur de l'Atlas. Paris, 1910.

Tarde, A. de. Les Villes du Maroc: Fez, Marrakech, Rabat. (Journal de l'Université des Annales, 15 Oct., 1 Nov., 1918.)

Windus. A Journey to Mequinez. London, 1721.

Printed in February 2023
by Rotomail Italia S.p.A., Vignate (MI) - Italy